WATER UNDER THE KEEL

WATER UNDER THE KEEL

Memories of the Sea

Robin Burnett

Book Guild Publishing

Sussex, England

First published in Great Britain in 2011 by
The Book Guild Ltd
Pavilion View
19 New Road
Brighton,
BN1 1UF

Typeset in Garamond by
Ellipsis Books Limited, Glasgow

Printed in Great Britain by
CPI Antony Rowe

A catalogue record for this book is available from
The British Library.

ISBN 978 1 84624 534 3

To the men of the Merchant Navy
and all seafarers, past and present.

Contents

Acknowledgements

I must first thank my wife, family and friends who have listened to various anecdotes about my life at sea and encouraged me over the years to write my memoirs. So finally here they are! I gleaned some help in tracking my voyages during the early days of my apprenticeship from my younger sister, Jane, who, while still at school, logged my progress across the world on one of those old *Daily Telegraph* maps. My eldest sister, Rosanna Stevenson, has assisted me in sifting, choosing and enhancing as necessary the heterogeneous collection of my own snapshots, ship postcards, faded transparencies and other ship photographs dating back more than fifty years. And I have been assisted in many ways by my wife Patricia.

I have been very impressed by those many lovers of the sea that I have since met or corresponded with, many of them with nostalgic memories of their own seafaring or sailing days. I have been enthralled by some priceless historical literature and the amazing and courageous exploits of men of the British Merchant Navy during the world wars, against which mine is but a humble tale. Every one of the many British shipping companies seems to have had its inspiring moments of drama and heroism. I have included historical information on one of the lesser-known tramp shipping companies, the Stanhope Steamship Company, to which I became an indentured apprentice in 1950. Telling an extraordinary story of the war record which led to Stanhope's post-war fleet of ships, this is based on a modest company brochure which I was given at the time I signed up, together with information gleaned from sailing with crew who had survived the Second World War and observations by my late uncle, Cdr James Burnett DSC, RN, who had sailed on convoy with a Stanhope ship.

I have included at some length an outline of the origins and amazing history of the Royal Mail Lines, inspired by Duncan Haws' *Royal Mail Line & Nelson Line* (1982), one of TCL Publications' Merchant Fleets series; by

Stuart Nicol's *MacQueen's Legacy: A History of the Royal Mail Line* and *Ships of the Royal Mail Line* (both 2001); by H.W. Leslie's *Royal Mail War Book* (1920), and by T.A. Bushell's *Eight Bells: The Royal Mail Lines War Story, 1939–45* (1950), from the latter of which I quote with the blessing of his daughters, Pat and June Bushell. I have to thank John Fordham for providing me with material on Royal Mail's war years. I am also very grateful to David Cobbold for putting me in touch with the Royal Mail Association newsletter edited by Bob Forrester, who has helped to fill in a few gaps.

The autobiographical material is taken direct from memory with assistance as to exact dates, ships and Captains' names from my Seaman's Record & Certificates of Discharge, issued on my entry into the Merchant Navy on 10th August 1950. Commonly known as a Discharge Book, this records the dates of signing on and off every voyage I made from apprentice to Chief Officer with its last entry in August 1968.

R.F. Burnett, B.Sc., MRINA, MNI

A Note on Nautical Measurements and Terms

Measurements are generally those employed at the time – that is, imperial, using feet (ft) and inches (in) – but I have occasionally used metres (m) as well. Distances are in nautical miles (nm), a unit of measurement that derives from the minutes of arc of latitude on the Earth's surface and standardised at 6,080 feet or 1,852 metres. A ship speed of 1 knot is 1 nautical mile per hour.

The different tonnages quoted for ships can be confusing. *Gross Tonnage* (gt) or *Gross Registered Tonnage* (grt) is a measure of the enclosed volume of the ship and hence its size by volume, measured at 100 cubic feet to the ton. *Displacement*, which is generally quoted for naval ships, is a measure of the weight of water displaced by the ship, hence the actual weight (1 ton = 35 cubic feet of salt water). *Deadweight tonnage* (dwt) is a measure of the cargo carrying tonnage of a ship in tons – that is the fully loaded displacement less the light (without cargo) displacement. Modern measure of weight in tonnes is the metric equivalent of these tonnages measured at 1 cubic metre of water to the tonne (1 tonne = 0.984 tons).

Some further ship terminology is explained on page 163.

And then I pressed the shell
Close to my ear
And listened well,
And straightway like a bell,
Came low and clear
The slow, sad murmur of the distant seas,

James Stephens,
The Shell

1

Schooldays

In the early years of the Second World War, my family were living in the quiet Sussex village of Rushlake Green, at The Old Forge, an idyllic tiled cottage, set in a typical Sussex country garden, a setting which appears little changed to this day. There I grew up with my two sisters and, as with most childhood memories, the sun seems to have been perpetually shining.

Certainly the sun was shining in the summer of 1940 and one of my most vivid recollections, at the age of seven, was seeing the Battle of Britain played out overhead in a pattern of white vapour trails across the brilliant blue skies; Hurricanes and Spitfires battled with the invading aircraft as they performed breathtaking ballets high in the sky. To us children, safely detached from grim reality, this was most exciting, but occasionally there would be the roar of a plane diving, a burst of machine-gun fire, the crump of a plane crashing or bang of a distant bomb unloaded by a retreating enemy plane. My mother frequently had to drag me indoors out of fear for my safety.

There were in reality some terrible moments, even in our sleepy village, during that time. Early one night a German bomber, heading for home, unloaded a bomb that fell directly onto a local bus which was showing its lights in the village. There was some tragic loss of life and several were wounded. At the time my mother was working for the Red Cross, along with Mrs Dunn, at Stone House at the top end of the green. Known as the 'Big House', this had been turned into an emergency medical centre to deal with the immediate crisis.

Another sign of the tragedy of war came unexpectedly one morning when I was lying in bed. We had a nanny from the village, Joyce Buss, a bright and friendly girl, working part-time to look after the three of us children. That morning she came into my room looking miserable and then threw herself sobbing uncontrollably on my bed. I had never seen a grown-up cry before

1

and this really shook me. My mother came in, put her arm round her and led her away. Later Mummy explained that Joyce's boyfriend was a sailor who had just been drowned along with many others when the pride of our fleet, the battleship HMS *Hood*, was sunk.

My Uncle James was a Lieutenant-Commander in the Royal Navy during those war years and sometimes stayed briefly with my parents at our Sussex home when on leave. He had been at Narvik and later commanded a corvette in the Western Approaches and escorted convoys destined for Malta. Although I of course understood very little of this, I was enthralled with the romantic dream of life in the Royal Navy, knowing nothing of the hardships involved, only that he needed to rest after his adventurous time at sea, the details of which were denied me. The expression 'Careless talk costs lives' was already being impressed upon us children.

As the danger of invasion became more real our family evacuated to Cornwall. My father was a schoolmaster by profession and was an old friend of the headmaster of the Brunswick boarding preparatory school. This private school claimed Winston Churchill as its most distinguished Old Boy, though I've never seen any reference made to that fact. Anyhow Brunswick was based at Haywards Heath in the heart of Sussex, which was very much in the firing line during the Battle of Britain and while fears of invasion grew. It was therefore decided to evacuate the entire school to Cornwall and in the winter of 1940–41 my father was called in to help with this project.

So, as a seven-year-old, I with my two sisters joined the relocated school at Michaelstow House near the village of St Tudy close to Bodmin Moor and the wild north Cornish coast. There both my father and mother taught, while my eight-year-old elder sister, Rosanna, joined in the classes and sports, including playing rugger, and Jane, just four, joined in with other younger brothers and sisters of the boys at the school. It was a wonderful place to be, and quite honestly those brief years were the only schooldays, always supposed to be 'the happiest days of your life', that I really did enjoy. We would be taken for walks on Bodmin Moor to picnic on the peaks of Rough Tor and Brown Willy, and on school holidays in the summer the school-boys would all be transported by hay cart to Tregardoc beach. This is a wild and dramatic spot, with high cliffs, caves and sparkling clean sand washed by rolling Atlantic waves. The beach could only be reached from an old farm down a bumpy track a mile from the coast road and then by coast-guard steps with rusted iron railings. When I visited there more than forty years later it had not changed one iota. On these days out, the understood rule for the school party was that once the tide came up to the edge of the cliffs we would have to pack up and re-embark into the tractor-driven hay carts. So, inevitably, most of the day was spent in building sand defences to keep the sea out for as long as possible. But one day we were ushered away with undue haste; a loose mine had been discovered floating close out to sea and the Home Guard were to be called in to blow it up with rifle fire.

To the great regret of my sisters and me, we moved back to the Home Counties two years later when my father took up a position as an English teacher at Whitgift School in Croydon. The family went to live at Caterham in Surrey and at the age of nine I was sent off to a boarding preparatory school near Hitchin.

This was a tough no-nonsense school where our autocratic headmaster believed in beating the boys, trousers down and with a leather belt, at every opportunity. Away from home for the first time, I was distinctly homesick, but Welbury School had its good points. It was hard work and strict discipline, but hard play as well. There were other consolations: school morale was high; we had an outdoor swimming pool, beautiful grounds, well-organised picnics and jolly parents' days; and I was in the Rugby XV, which always did well against other schools. Despite the war we were extremely well fed. The roast potatoes were a legend; no matter that we were sent out during class hours to harvest these potatoes from the neighbouring farm for hours of back-breaking work, which was, after all, preferable to Latin.

For the main part we were well insulated from the war in Hertfordshire, although there was one occasion when a Lancaster bomber limping home, having been damaged after a leaflet raid over Berlin, crashed in a nearby field. The ambulances and police had already been but, before a proper guard could be put on the wreck, we boys had swarmed all over it. I came away with rolls of silver foil, of the type that was scattered to distract enemy radar, and a charred leaflet written in German. This showed what the Nazis had done to our cities with graphic photographs of London and Coventry suffering during the Blitz and promised retaliation. One or two boys came away with live ammunition and were soundly beaten when their souvenirs were discovered.

At Caterham during the holidays, it became a different story for, just south of London, we were caught in the heart of the V1 Doodlebug raids; we heard the buzz of many of these approaching, day or night. Then the eerie silence when the engine stopped before the flying bomb hit the ground and exploded. The family would take turns in sleeping in pairs in our Anderson shelter in the garden. There was also an incendiary raid one night which set fire to the large Congregational church right opposite our home. Although I was away at school at the time, I was regaled later by Rosanna and Jane with vivid pictures of flames leaping high into the air on the other side of the road and illuminating all around. My father was working flat out as an ARP warden almost every night during this time.

A sad feature of the war was that my paternal grandparents were separated throughout. My father's family lived in Guernsey where my grandfather, Herbert, grew pink carnations commercially in his market garden on the island's south coast, having introduced a new strain to the island. Both my father and uncle grew up in Guernsey, before being sent for schooling in England, to Haileybury and Dartmouth respectively. At the outbreak of war Herbert, realising the danger of invasion, came to the mainland to find a home for the two of them, but before he could bring over his wife, and while a mass evacuation of the inhabitants was still underway amid great confusion as to who should go or stay, the Germans invaded on 1st July 1940. My grandmother, Ethel, was stuck on the island for the duration but she did have the forethought to bury the family silver in the garden.

German soldiers were billeted in her house, but she was a tough character and by all accounts she kept them in order, even applying a strict curfew at night. But life was hard and food scarce. Ethel had the additional problem of being a heavy smoker, and cigarettes were a rare luxury. By sheer chance, when I visited Guernsey while on leave many years later, I saw, in the German underground hospital, by then turned into a rather dank museum, a framed page of the local *Gazette* which included a personal ad put in by Ethel Burnett offering to exchange a pair of her evening shoes for cigarettes. When the two grandparents were finally reunited in England after the war, Herbert was a frail, white-bearded but dignified old man living with my parents in Sussex, and it was not long before he died.

Back at my prep school I did particularly well at athletics, learnt to swim the length of the pool underwater and got into the rugger team. My cricket, though, left a lot to be desired, and I usually ended up fielding at long stop – something to do with being what was called a 'shifted sinistrel'. I had smudged my copybook too often when writing with my left hand, and I never knew whether I would do better to bat, bowl or throw with left or right hand, and as a result proved pretty incompetent with both.

While out playing rugby in the winter with the wind whistling in my ears and rain or sleet in my face, I would often dream of being at sea and would imagine myself on the bridge of a ship battling the wind and waves. The words of John Masefield's 'Sea Fever' seemed to ring in my ears:

I must down to the seas again, for the call of the running tide
Is a wild call and a clear call that may not be denied;
And all I ask is a windy day with the white clouds flying,
And the flung spray and the blown spume, and the sea-gulls crying.

Of course in reality my only experience of the sea had been playing and swimming on the beaches at Pevensey and Birling Gap, and on the wild coast of Cornwall, as a small child.

Latin and Maths were taught at school with a positively physical intensity by a Dickensian tyrant of a teacher who had a particular penchant for twisting my ear when my declensions faltered. But the result was that at the age of twelve I could translate Virgil and Caesar with ease, and had taken algebra and geometry in my stride. After a year in the top form I sailed through the academic entrance examination for Dartmouth, which could have set me on a career in the Royal Navy. However, this was a very competitive examination, permitting only about one in eight of the entrants to be accepted. Included in the selection process were interviews and medicals at the Admiralty inflicted on all those thirteen-year olds who had passed the written exams.

Faced across the table by the admirals I thought I had done well enough, but they had many tricks up their sleeves. It was considered a great help to have had relatives in the Navy, which I had on both sides of the family; a great-uncle on my mother's side, Sidney Selby-Hall, had been an admiral of distinction in the First World War. But among my mistakes, when told to tie the ends of a piece of string together, I clumsily tied a granny knot instead of a reef knot. Whether this was the defining error I couldn't say, but it must have been a close thing for three weeks later my parents received a letter from the Lords of the Admiralty indicating that I could possibly be selected, depending on whether some other lad, chosen ahead of me, succeeded in an appeal against his medical examination. After a further two or three weeks of anxious waiting during the long summer holidays I learnt that I had failed to qualify. So, after being given a choice of trying for a place on a training ship or a more conventional all-round education by my patient parents, I chose the latter and was duly sent to the Oratory School, a small English Catholic public school near Reading which had a reputation for turning out well-mannered young gentlemen and included among the pupils the sons of several European and Latin diplomats.

Life at The Oratory was easier and more pleasant than at my prep school but in those early post-war years the school had the distinction of being the smallest public school in England with only about ninety pupils. The school had been relocated from a mansion taken over by the BBC at Caversham outside Reading and was struggling for survival. The teaching standards were not high, particularly in the scientific subjects, for which good staff could not be found. We did not have a very good sporting record either, but there was considerable enthusiasm for cricket, ours being one of the select few schools which traditionally played an annual cricket match at Lords. Ours was a one-day match against Beaumont eagerly attended by the parents and boys of both schools as well as Old Boys and their wives and girlfriends. Indeed it was a very smart occasion, though, of course, the ground was only partially filled. As an Old Boy in later years I only once managed to get to Lords for this match when on leave from the sea but eventually the commercialisation of cricket spelt an inevitable end to the fixture. However, under the tutelage of our very erudite headmaster and a brilliant Classics master, we at least managed to put up a chess team which could beat all the surrounding schools. Being fast on my feet I also played on the wing in the Colts rugby team but did not have the size and strength to make the 1st XV.

Although I did well enough to achieve matriculation at the age of fifteen, I then struggled with Higher Certificate Maths and Chemistry over the next two years. At sixteen, my parents arranged for me to go abroad for the first time on an exchange during the school summer holidays to stay with the Armstad family in a village of that name on the shores of Lake Lucerne. Ostensibly I was supposed to be improving my French which I would be taking for Higher Certificate, although, as the main language at Lucerne was Swiss German, I made little progress.

Staying by Lake Lucerne I really took to the water for the first time; I was enthralled by the leisurely white paddle-steamers with their tall funnels as they steamed round the smooth blue waters stopping at every landing stage to take on the local people and their goods bound to and from Lucerne. I thought what a wonderful life it would be to be the skipper of such a ship! Of course it was not always calm and there were some magnificent electric storms. The violence of thunderstorms can best be appreciated when seen over water, which reflects the lightning and tumult of the sky above. I was supposed to be getting to know the country a bit but, being left to myself most days, I spent many hours taking the Armstads' rowing boat around the lake, fishing and stopping off at any suitable cove for a swim and a picnic. It was too soon after the war for this area to have developed into a major holiday resort, though there were some pre-war grand hotels around the shore and in the hills overlooking the lake. Our own little village of Armstad was in the main a farming community and had an old cable lift running up to the top of the hills above that was mainly used by farmers and woodsmen. The lift was simply operated by gravity, having a tank under the seating platform of each of two cars; the upper tank would be filled with rain water and this would be emptied when the car reached the lower station. So all it required was a brake mechanism to control the descent.

Rather to my own surprise, and in retrospect clearly due in part to not having worked hard enough during my two years in the sixth form, I failed the Dartmouth Special Entry exam at the age of seventeen. My father was very disappointed with me and, back from school for the summer holiday, the question of my future loomed.

It would have been nice to go on to university, but I had always said I wanted to go to sea and I suddenly I found myself facing an instant decision, and the outcome was rather forced on me. By chance an acquaintance of my parents knew a millionaire shipowner, Jack Billmeir, chairman and principal shareholder of the Stanhope Steamship Co. He suggested that I apply to his company, which proved to be only too ready to offer me a four-year apprenticeship immediately. In fact, after a brief interview in the Bishopsgate offices of the company, I was appointed to one of their ships, a tanker named *Stanwell*. I was given an impressive list of uniform and seagoing clothing requirements, including a greatcoat, cap and badge, blue uniform, white shirts, white tropical uniforms, oilskin, sou'wester, white duck shoes, black shoes, sea boots and many other things, for which my father had to dig deep. But were they to know it, as a mere apprentice in a tramp shipping company, most of my time would in reality be spent in dungarees or shorts, sweatshirts or boiler suit – in other words, in plain working gear, for I was to be, for the most part, cheap hard labour.

So in early August 1950 I was whisked away as an indentured apprentice in the Merchant Navy. It was a dramatic culture shock to be catapulted within a month from being a sixth-form pupil at an English public school in the fine setting of the Berkshire countryside to finding oneself sailing the world in a tramp ship and being treated as the lowest form of life aboard.

About to go to sea, August 1950.

2

I Go to Sea

So it was that on 14th August 1950, a the age of seventeen, I travelled down to Falmouth by train, very self-conscious in my new Merchant Navy cadet's uniform and clutching my suitcases and canvas kitbag. There, on a fine summer's day, I was collected at the old harbour from the stone steps over which the water still laps today. My new berth, the oil tanker *Stanwell*, could be seen swinging lazily from her anchor chain out in the bay, as the ship's Third Mate motored over to the steps with a couple of able seamen to pick me up in the ship's lifeboat.

When I signed on as apprentice with the Stanhope Steamship Co. in 1950, the company had a fleet of nineteen cargo ships and oil tankers, of which the tankers *Stanwell* and her sister, *Stanmore*, were the most recently built. (In Appendix 1 I describe the Stanhope fleet history through the Second World War). The *Stanwell*, American-built towards the end of the war, could carry 16,000 tons of fuel oil. She seemed enormous as, stripped of cargo and ballast, her sides rode some 30 feet high above the water. The black topsides and red boot-topping paintwork of her welded steel hull were already pit-marked and streaming with rust as she awaited drydocking for repairs and repainting. High canvas ventilator cowls, flapping in the wind as though gasping for breath, were suspended over her now-empty oil tanks. So I clambered out of the lifeboat and climbed the accommodation ladder of my first ship, expectant but apprehensive about what the future might hold in store for me.

Falmouth Bay is one of the world's largest natural harbours, and picturesque too with hills rolling down to the water and its old town clustered around the quayside. The commercial side of the port specialised in drydocking, cleaning and repairing ships. One of its principal customers at the time was the British Tanker Co., a company boasting more than a hundred ships, the largest single company then flying the Red Ensign.

My first ship, the tanker *Stanwell*. *(Author's ink sketch 1950)*

That week in August *Stanwell*'s cargo tanks were being cleaned by shore gangs and ventilated to gas-free them prior to the ship undergoing routine repairs alongside to pipes, pumps, valves, bulkheads and cargo heating coils. It was very common for cargo tanks to leak from one to another and this could be a problem when loading different 'parcels' of oil products, although tankers used for tramping, or picking up cargoes as they became available, usually tended to carry full cargoes of heavy crude or fuel oil. The cargo heating coils which wound their way across the bottom of the tanks, and through which steam was passed, were essential to soften the sludge that formed at the bottom of a tank full of heavy crude oil, so that it could be pumped out. But these coiled pipes could leak at their joints and hence needed regular overhaul.

Ten days after I joined the *Stanwell* we steamed out of Falmouth to load a cargo of crude oil from the British Petroleum refinery at Abadan in Iran. I was soon made to realise how out of place my smart blue uniform with gold buttons was in a tramp shipping company. In reality, apprentices provided these companies with a useful form of cheap labour. We were paid just £6 10s. a month but we did get three square meals a day and had no expenses to worry about. I shared a cabin with my fellow apprentice, 'Dick' Turpin, who was also on his first voyage to sea. Our cabin had two bunks, a settee, desk, chair and en-suite shower and toilet. These American-built ships were sensibly outfitted with fire safety to the fore but were not exactly aesthetically pleasing, there being no wood interior fittings and furniture, all grey steel in the cabins with synthetic upholstery. Nevertheless the accommodation was comfortable and in this respect I was very lucky not to have been posted to one of the company's older coal-burning cargo tramps.

Dick and I were initially put on daywork under the bosun, doing manual jobs on deck with the other sailors, these being graded as ABs (able seamen), ordinary seamen, and deckhands. On first crossing the Bay of Biscay in a cargo ship or tanker, without of course having the benefit of such luxuries as stabilisers, any new crew member would begin to find out how affected he was likely to be by seasickness. Our first crossing was no exception; faced by menacing grey Atlantic rollers, I was not actually sick but developed the most uncomfortable headache as we pitched into the hostile grey head seas, the ship's bow rising and falling over a range of 30 to 40 feet, with every now and again a sickening thud as our hull slammed into the head swell. The bosun, determined to initiate us quickly and, I suspect, with an element of sadism, had us stowing the ship's mooring ropes down in the forepeak, a deep locker under the bow, where the pitching motion was at its most violent. We fell about while trying to get our sea legs and, with the blood draining from our heads each time the bow rose up, the two of us struggled to coil the heavy manila mooring ropes. These ropes measured 8 inches in circumference, and were manhandled down into the locker by the sailors from above, so that they coiled down around us like elongated snakes.

Normally we did up to eight hours a day work with the sailors between Monday and Friday, also to Saturday midday. Daywork regularly commenced with washing down using saltwater hoses at 0700 hours. Traditionally all decks were supposed to be clean and dry by 0800 hours. Then after breakfast we cadets would be cleaning brass on the bridge, chipping rust, scraping bulwarks, or tarring and painting decks.

Traditionally also, the compass binnacle and two engine-room telegraphs, which were the means for manually transmitting engine orders from full ahead to stop and full astern, were made of solid brass and had to be kept shining bright. We also attempted to clean the ship's bell on the forecastle before arriving in port, but this was always so tarnished that we resorted to using the Board of Trade lime juice – very rough stuff which was still issued to all British ships as a cure for scurvy. This quickly dissolved the verdigris on the bell; though heaven knows what it would have done to our stomachs if we'd actually taken it.

Frequently we worked out in the blazing sun, as *Stanwell* made her way through the progressively hotter Mediterranean, Red Sea and Persian Gulf. How grateful we were for the American practice of providing iced-water fountains on board their ships, as we sweated on deck under the merciless sun of the Persian Gulf that August, typically chipping rust from deck plates with small hammers and plastering red-lead protective coatings over the steel.

A highlight of the crew's day was always breakfast, when the dayworkers met up with those who had been on watches during the night for a mammoth meal designed to appeal to all tastes; this consisted of grapefruit, cereal or porridge, curry and rice, bacon and egg and finally flapjack and syrup.

When off duty the cadets had to do correspondence courses in seamanship and navigation for submission to the company's marine superintendent at the end of the voyage. Meanwhile under the bosun we were taught how to make every conceivable splice and knot for wires and ropes. The deckhands treated this skill with pride and one would never be considered a seaman until one had learnt to call everything by its proper name, coil ropes, tie the right knots, and throw heaving lines to mooring boats or quayside so that they uncoiled in the air without tangling. We also soon became very proficient at the more prosaic task of scaling ship's plates and painting ship. We learnt to paint quickly and proficiently without leaving 'holidays' (spaces) or making 'curtains' (runs) on the ship's plating.

One job with which we were entrusted as apprentices was to replace all the lifeboat stores of food when necessary. Board of Trade rules required the lifeboats' hard rations of ship's biscuits, barley sugar and condensed milk to be renewed every two years; so the two of us got the new supply from the bosun's store, stowed them in the boat lockers and, for perks, were able to help ourselves to the out-of-date rations. The condensed milk we often drank straight from the can but we also found it made delicious caramel if boiled up in its tins in the officers' pantry.

After a few weeks the two of us were put on 'watches', there being three crew to a watch under the Watchkeeping Officer. Watch duty combined manual work, standby, helming and lookout duty. As cadets we found ourselves on the 4–8 watch morning and evening, where we learnt to steer under the watchful eye of the Chief Officer. Steering a large ship from the wheelhouse is not difficult in principle; it just requires total concentration to prevent the ship veering off course, while one stands – no sitting ever allowed – behind the wheel and watches the gyro compass for up to two hours on end. If one's mind strayed the tell-tale click of the swinging compass rose would quickly alert the officer on the bridge. The stint at the helm during the lonely hours from 0400 and 0600, with the concentration that it required when all one wanted to do was sleep, was to me the most unpleasant job on board ship. I preferred cleaning the bilges any day. But with the dawn light, the ship started to come to life, and one felt how wonderful it was to come off duty for a mug of strong hot tea. The sailors preferred to drink tea sweetened with condensed milk, thick and 'strong enough to stand a spoon up in', out of PLA mugs 'borrowed' from the Port of London Authority. Sipping this hot brew as daylight crept over the horizon, we would watch the changing yellow, pink and green lights of the sky mirrored in the water all around, never tiring of the magic of dawn at sea.

We cadets had also to learn to use the Morse lamp for signalling other ships, to identify flag signals, and to read semaphore (though the latter form of communication was no longer used in practice). We also became familiar with the basic navigation skills: taking triangular cross bearings or running fixes from landmarks by measuring angles using the compass repeaters on the bridge wings, or taking azimuth bearings of the sun and stars in order to check the errors of the magnetic and gyro compasses. It is surprisingly simple to calculate from the nautical almanac at what precise bearing the sun will rise and set (the angle of amplitude) in any specific latitude and so compare it with the visual bearings shown by the magnetic and gyro compasses and note the relevant compass error to the nearest degree. Sunrise and sunset bearings were taken, not as one might expect when the sun was seen on the horizon, but at the moment when the bottom edge of the sun's orb appeared to be one-half its own diameter above the horizon, this to allow for refraction. Then, as we became more proficient we learnt celestial position fixing by taking sun and star sights with the sextant. Star sights had to be taken at twilight over the moments when both the horizon and the brighter (first-magnitude) stars could be seen through the sextant telescope and mirror.

Star and sun sights required great accuracy in measurement and timing for, in those days, this was the accepted means of fixing the ship's position when out of sight of land; yet an error of one-sixtieth of a degree in altitude, or one second in time as taken from the ship's chronometer, could make a difference of one mile in positioning on the Earth's sphere. The chronometer, slung in gimbals so it remained unaffected by the ship's rolling and pitching, and checked daily by regular time signals from Greenwich, was thus crucial to any ship's navigation.

I felt the excitement when, after about four days into my first voyage, we reached the Strait of Gibraltar among a fleet of converging shipping; also some relief at being clear of the Atlantic swell. I was somewhat disappointed by my first sight of Gibraltar as we passed through the Strait. Seen from out in the open sea, 'The Rock' hardly stands out from the surrounding Spanish mountains as it had always seemed to in pictures. But we were now in the Mediterranean, and there was good weather, blue seas, flying fish and dolphins often playing around the ship. Through the Sicilian Channel we saw the island of Pantelleria to starboard and distant Mount Etna to port, then lower lying Gozo and Malta before some days later approaching Port Said and the Arab world.

Our trip through the Suez Canal provided a colourful break in routine with, after two weeks at sea, our first delivery of mail from home arriving in the shipping agent's boat, as we took on water and stores, and experienced the hustle and bustle of the 'bumboats' in Port Said. The crews of these boats were some of the world's most persuasive salesman and could sell every conceivable souvenir, from leather goods, mats, beads and potions to the traditional dirty books and postcards. They could also, we were warned, steal the shirt off your back.

In the early 1950s our ship still had a British or French pilot to guide us through the canal, while a large searchlight was lashed to the forecastle to show the way at night. It was a remarkable sensation to be gliding through the canal within a stone's throw of the desert on either side. There were still British soldiers stationed there at the time and they would wave and shout to us as we sailed past. Our ship travelled in convoy and anchored in the Bitter Lakes, to allow the northbound convoy to pass. This gave us our one much appreciated opportunity to lower the gangway for a swim. Then after anchoring at Suez and disembarking the pilot and shore crew, we were back to routine again but now accompanied by an oven-like breeze off the desert curling up small white crests on the brilliant blue seas. There was always a constant stream of ships up and down the Red Sea, passing within a mile or two of each other; these were dominated by tankers of the British Tanker Co. running to and from the Gulf, but there were also many cargo ships and passenger liners trafficking from the East.

Sailors always took a great interest in every other deep-sea ship they passed. Some would be carrying crews from the same home port, be it Glasgow, Liverpool, Middlesbrough or Swansea. Ships of the same company when passing each other would ceremoniously dip their ensigns and blow their whistles in acknowledgement. There was always a good deal of critical comment among the sailors on tramp cargo ships as to whether ships of another shipping company were most importantly good feeders, made short or long voyages, had well-maintained ships, were happy ships and to what degree they indulged in 'bullshit', or in other words expected a smart uniformed turnout with disciplines approaching those of the Royal Navy.

A sort of class system was understood between shipping lines of the British Merchant Navy, the Orient liners being the aristocracy, then an upper class of other cargo and passenger liner companies such as P&O, British India, Union Castle and Royal Mail, followed by a host of regular cargo liners such as Clan Line and Ellermans (then the largest privately owned cargo company), the various tanker fleets, of which the white-hulled Onassis tankers were probably the smartest at that time, and finally the working-class tramp ships based on ports such as London, Liverpool, Swansea and Cardiff, of which the Stanhope cargo ships were typical examples. There

14

were also an increasing number of London Greek tramps owned by million-aires such as Onassis, Niarchos, Leonidas and others, all taking advantage of the post-war boom in shipping rates by running older ships to death. These had been mostly mass-produced in wartime America and were almost ready for the scrapyard, but nonetheless able to pay for themselves in just two or three voyages during the height of the shipping boom.

The length of a British crew's stay on board normally lasted until a ship returned from deep sea to a port in home waters, but, according to the Board of Trade terms under which we 'signed on', this could last for any length of time up to two years if the shipowner so wished. The shipping lines doing regular short voyages were naturally the most popular among crews, but, unless contracted to a specific company, many sailors would sign on any ship available from the labour 'pool', after having taken as much leave as suited them. These periods of leave were often in practice governed by how long their cash lasted after being 'paid off' from the previous voyage.

East of Suez the landscape on either side of the Red Sea, through the Straits of Hormuz and up the Persian Gulf, became one of uniform and monotonous barren hills, all of a purplish hue in the distance while, nearer to, the sea dazzled under cloudless skies. In the bright clear blue sea porpoises often played in front of the ship's bow and small flying fish would leap out of the foaming wash, sometimes even landing on deck to be hosed away the next morning. Although we didn't try eating these fish which were not much bigger than sprats, I'm told that they could be very tasty.

In the Indian Ocean I saw waterspouts for the first time. These are common enough but nonetheless a remarkable sight. The waterspout is a gyrating column of mist, spray and water, produced by the action of a whirl-wind on the sea surface with a squall cloud immediately above it. It develops an hourglass shape, thinnest at approximately mid-height where, when its power is spent, it will break and subside. Waterspouts move across the sea with the clouds and we would take deliberate avoiding action because of the damage they can cause.

When in the Persian Gulf we frequently came across Arab dhows. These are open sailing cargo boats with a single large sail of a type which has not changed in hundreds or perhaps thousands of years. To us, poorly lit or unlit at night, they were something of a navigational hazard. It was, however, accepted custom to stop and give water to these dhows when they were found becalmed far from land if they waved to us for assistance.

Our destination, the oil refinery at Abadan, was approached under pilotage up the Shatt al-Arab River. We had a moment of excitement, that first voyage, when our ship completely blacked out; the ship's machinery being turbo-electric powered, the engines, steering gear and winches were all taken out together. The only possible action in such a situation was to drop the anchor. As a normal procedure we always had an anchor party on standby forward when in landlocked waterways so, on this occasion, as the chain rattled out and our 400ft long ship swung to face the current, our stern bore down on an anchored Iranian gunboat, much to the alarm of the solitary Arab crewman on her afterdeck. It was a very close shave. He watched helpless as the ensign staff at our stern actually swept away a line of crew's washing hung out over the other vessel's poop deck, so close did we come to collision. The alarm on the face of the crewman was comic and I'm afraid our crew saw the funny side, much to the indignation of the Iranian crew. Still, we had a local pilot on board and no international incident ensued. Pilots who are familiar with the location are taken aboard in all port areas and, although they do not theoretically supersede the Captain's responsibility, they do in fact con the ship.

The refinery at Abadan was most striking for its huge cylindrical oil tanks, with gases burning off in great flares from a multitude of shining steel chimneys, a blaze of lights everywhere, and the sickly, almost intoxicating, smell of gas evaporating from crude oil which we soon came to know so well. With pipelines connected to our manifold of pipes on the cargo deck, and tank valves opened, the oil was pumped into our tanks at a furious rate so that you could almost see the vessel settling in the water under her 16,000-ton load. We were glad to be away again and were homeward bound in forty-eight hours.

On the homeward voyage the motion of the loaded ship was remarkably different from the ballasted outward voyage. The hull was now lower in the water by 20 feet or so; load-line rules permitted just a few feet of freeboard above the sea surface, the oil cargo itself being lighter than water and so providing the necessary buoyancy. For maximum profit tankers invariably loaded to the deepest permissible draught to the last inch. Underway, this meant that whenever seas were rough the decks became very wet with spray and even took on solid water or 'green seas'. Hence the need for a catwalk, more correctly known as the flying bridge, which was the only safe way of getting from the midship accommodation and wheelhouse to the accommodation block aft, which contained galley, mess rooms, pump room and engine-room access. Even so one frequently had to run the gauntlet along the catwalk at mealtimes trying to keep dry, and it was not uncommon to have to rig safety lines on the foredeck when working there. One visible effect of the deep draught under a full load was the surprising number of flying fish which landed up on deck.

At just over 16,500 tons deadweight, *Stanwell* was an average size of tanker for those days. We had twenty-seven cargo tanks, in nine rows of three; each row comprising two wing tanks and a centre tank, four of the rows being forward of the bridge and five aft. Some of the latest Onassis Olympic big white sleek tankers could carry about 20,000 tons but few were larger than that, as this was before the days of supertankers.

The explosion in size that lead to the construction of half-million-ton tankers was not to come until the 1960s and 70s. Initially the closure of the Suez Canal following the '67 Arab–Israeli War meant that tankers had to sail round the Cape. This was the catalyst which was much later to lead to the demand, with economy in size, for very large crude carriers (VLCCs) typically with a cargo capacity of 250,000 tons or more.

We arrived back in Swansea to discharge our cargo of crude oil, paying off and signing on a new crew before the end of October 1950, then set off for Abadan again, but this time on a much longer voyage to deliver another oil cargo to the River Plate. After many days of monotonous watch-keeping at sea we called all too briefly at Cape Town for bunkers; we had a short run ashore from our oil jetty, just long enough to note Table Mountain, shrouded in cloud, to observe the colourful mixture of colonial elegance and poor homesteads, and the contrast between the day-to-day life of the white and black man during that period of apartheid. Then we were away to cross 3,700 miles of the South Atlantic before entering the River Plate to pump our black cargo ashore at La Plata. My first experience of South America did not offer a lot to see in the wide estuary of the River Plate with its flat coastlines but the sight of laid-up Sunderland flying boats like wounded birds with clipped wings, and the mainmast of the German battle cruiser *Graf Spee* still showing above water, stand out in my memory. We made the long trip back to Abadan and then to Swansea with another cargo, arriving back after five months away from home.

Our next voyage offered interest and variety. We had a very welcome break in Palermo, where the ship went for extensive drydocking for all of three weeks, work being cheaper there. These tankers had been welded together in a hurry during the war and there was a never-ending repair list. There was not a lot for us cadets to do on board, though we still kept deck watches each day. Palermo was a big industrial port and city, not exactly a tourist resort, but I went to see the famous catacombs and to admire the magnificent golden mosaics in the medieval cathedral at Monreale.

Thence we went to the Mediterranean ports of Sidon, a cargo to Port-de-Bouc in France and back through the very scenic Messina Straits which separate the toe of Italy from Sicily, to Tripoli, and another cargo to cross the Atlantic to Philadelphia, where we loaded fuel oil for the small naval port of Invergordon in Scotland. This involved heading north round Cape Wrath where, while doing my hour's lookout duty one dark night, I experienced for the first time the eerie green, yellow and blue flashing Northern Lights. From the shelter of Invergordon we then made a coastal voyage via the North Sea and English Channel to our home port of Swansea where the ship paid off on 3rd October 1951. I took two weeks' leave with my parents before being ordered to sign on a new British-built cargo ship MV *Stanhope*.

3

The Cargo Vessel Stanhope

And now the storm-blast came, and he
Was tyrannous and strong:
He struck with his o'ertaking wings,
and chased us south along.

The Rime of the Ancient Mariner, Samuel Taylor Coleridge

After taking a spell of leave at my parents' new home at Tilford near Farnham in Surrey, I was sent to London's West India Docks that October 1951, where I signed on the 6,000 gt motor ship *Stanhope*, newly built at Burntisland on the north-east coast. It was a wonderful relief to be working on a cargo ship after the tanker, which had spent so much time at sea and so little in port. In a tanker virtually our only shoreside contact during a voyage was with oil refineries or merely oil jetties extending out to sea, as if to keep us as far offshore as possible.

On board *Stanhope* in the London Docks with my mother, uncle and father 1951.

19

With engine room and accommodation amidships and single screw propulsion, MV *Stanhope* was a standard five-hold dry-cargo vessel with a tweendeck throughout, typical of that time, and equipped for handling cargo with 5-ton derricks at each hatch, steam winches and one 20-ton heavy lift derrick abaft the foremast.

My voyage in *Stanhope* turned out to be remarkable in that, during nine months at sea, we called at only five ports, namely Sydney, Vancouver, Bombay, Dairen in Manchuria, then homeward to Hamburg. Outward bound from the London Docks to Sydney, Australia, we carried a full cargo of Morris Minor cars. These were stowed in crates in all five holds and three high on deck, one thousand in all. Being built for economy with a single Doxford diesel engine, our ship had no need to refuel on the way; so we sailed down the Atlantic coast and round the Cape of Good Hope direct for Sydney, a voyage that took us forty-two days, certainly the longest single period that I ever spent at sea. Apart from a distant view of Table Mountain to port as we rounded the Cape, we had never a sight of land once clear of European waters.

Occasionally we saw whales spouting, but just once did I experience the majestic sight, barely half a mile away, of a pair leaping up from the water and plunging back into the foam with a flurry of their tails as they followed in the waves created by our wash.

Albatrosses were another awesome sight, slender birds with a wingspan of up to ten feet, as they sometimes followed in our wake, gliding gracefully on the air currents of the Southern Ocean. One morning, when our ship was heaving in fairly rough weather, an albatross clipped the foremast rigging with a wing and fell to the deck. As a seabird it was unable to take off again from the steel deck and lurched about, frightened and physically sick. To see the disorientated creature on its way the bosun formed a chain of sailors across the foredeck to usher it to the ship's side where the bird fell to the water and was able to fly away again in our wake.

It was not all plain sailing, however. Our engine broke down while we were in the 'roaring forties' well south of Cape Leeuwin, off the tip of the Australian south-west coast, being set on an easterly course to pass south of Tasmania. Teething troubles are not uncommon in a new ship, but with a heavy swell running and a strong force 6–7 following wind, we could not have chosen a more uncomfortable place. At about 0900 on that grey stormy day, as *Stanhope* lost way she inevitably broached beam on to the wind and swell, so that we started to roll heavily, about 25 degrees to each side. In these unpleasant conditions, the engineers struggled throughout the day to get the engine repaired.

Meanwhile, on deck, under the continuing shift of weight of the cargo crates from side to side with each roll, the restraining wire lashings began to cut into the sides of the wooden crates. As a result these wires became looser so that the crates started to move, until the whole three-high deck cargo of crates dragged alternately to port and starboard with ominous grinding noises at each roll of the ship. It was too dangerous for the crew to go on deck to attempt to secure the lashings, if that were even possible, so we just watched from the deckhouse, waited and prayed for engine power to be restored. Under the relentless vertical and sideways pressures of the cargo with each roll, the lower tier of crates began to give and settle lower, while the second tier were also soon beginning to break up. Our cargo of brand-new Morris Minors was being destroyed before our eyes. Eventually the lower tier of crates collapsed to just about three feet high, the frames of the cars being individually squashed down between their wheels.

At about 1600 to everyone's relief the Chief Engineer called from the voice pipe in the engine room to the bridge where Captain Williams was anxiously pacing and I was standing by the wheel. The Captain's concern was of course not only with the cargo but the safety of the drifting ship as it is not good to be without power in a storm. Now at last the engine throbbed and the funnel gave out a cloud of black smoke as we were able to turn slowly into the wind; the heavy rolling motion was replaced by

Weather damage to *Stanhope*'s deck cargo of three tiers of crated Morris cars.
(Author's photo 1952)

21

moderate pitching into the seas as we resumed our eastward course with a following sea. *Stanhope* arrived in Sydney a few days later with a deck cargo of splintered crates. I don't believe that there was one of those 200 cars stowed on deck which was undamaged and most were certainly written off. However, that was for the shippers and their insurers to sort out; we had done all we could and there is always an implicit risk in carrying deck cargo.

Sydney provided us with a marvellous two-week break over Christmas while we discharged our cargo and then loaded general cargo for Vancouver. The natural harbour of Sydney lived up to its scenic reputation and at that time there were not many high-rise buildings to spoil the vista. I walked through the Botanical Gardens, an oasis in the heart of the city close to the north side of Sydney Harbour Bridge. The gardens had been developed on land where the early settlers had channelled precious freshwater streams to grow wheat. Winding red-earth paths took one through and under lush subtropical vegetation, orange- and red-flowering shrubs and tree ferns. There, sitting on some rocks, the now-famous Opera House not having then been built, I had a go at drawing the bridge in my sketchbook, but, defeated by the awkward perspective presented by this imposing structure, I never quite finished the drawing; I still have the sketch with me today as a reminder of that voyage.

On a boiling-hot Christmas Day, we incongruously ate our traditional turkey and Christmas pudding, then those of us not on duty headed for Bondi Beach. Before leaving Sydney we also threw a New Year's party on board with the many acquaintances we had made ashore, who enjoyed the novelty of coming aboard while we lay out at anchor in that beautiful natural harbour.

From Sydney course was set straight out to cross the Pacific Ocean, for another uninterrupted twenty-eight days at sea, while we lived in our own small world just keeping routine watches, carrying out maintenance duties and doing weekly lifeboat drills, with hardly a sight of another ship. One would have dearly loved a stopover in the South Sea Islands which we passed by so near. But we re-crossed the Equator to the northern hemisphere without incident. Finally as we approached the coast of British Columbia, a full twenty-four hours before sighting land, the scent of pine trees became clearly discernible. We approached the port of Vancouver up the Juan de Fuca Strait round the tip of Vancouver Island. This was heavily wooded with conifers on both sides and the oily smooth waterway was busy with tugs towing bundles of logs. On a wet and misty February morning we made our landfall.

Vancouver is another scenic natural harbour approached by passing under the Lions Gate suspension bridge. Again, we found it a very friendly city, and visitors would pour on board. Although in port one had to work cargo duty, we two cadets alternating watch about, for twelve hours a day, I took time to see as much of the surroundings as I could on foot. I walked around the parks with their giant redwood trees and the totem poles, and across the spectacular Lions Gate Bridge to the foot of Grouse Mountain where a cable car took me to the snowy summit. This was the early days of the development of ski resorts and Grouse Mountain had the first, and at that time only, ski run in the area.

While our ship was in Vancouver that early February of 1952 we were shocked to receive the sad news of the death of King George V1. The local newspaper headlines read: 'The King is dead; long live the Queen.' The great concern shown by the people of British Columbia was not surprising if one recalls that only three months earlier Princess Elizabeth, accompanied by the Duke of Edinburgh, had made a very popular State Visit to Canada, touring the country, in place of her father, the King, who was already ailing.

At Vancouver we were loaded down with grain, which was poured in from silos. Then it was a long passage across the Pacific through the Singapore Straits and round Ceylon to Bombay, where our cargo was discharged, contrastingly, in the most labour-intensive manner. Teams of wharfies came aboard and squatted in the holds where they sewed the grain up in individual bags. A netful of bags would then be swung ashore on the ship's derricks. This process would take about ten days to complete. There was nothing too much to worry about while discharging and plenty of time to wander ashore when off duty.

Bombay was hot, dusty, colourful and noisy; the visitor is always dismayed by the number of beggars, many of them maimed, who line the quayside and streets. There were always men squatting in the streets ready to entertain for a few rupees. A favourite trick was to produce a snake from a sack. This reptile would sway and hiss menacingly, and could be charmed with music, but when the entertainer had a sufficient audience a mongoose would be produced and, in a fight to the death, would always kill the snake by biting its neck.

On the waterfront was the famous Gateway to India. Another feature on the waterfront which stuck in my memory was a flat-roofed tower over which the vultures circled constantly. We were told that the Parsis laid the bodies of their dead there for the vultures to pick their bones.

One oasis of colonial civilisation was the all-white Breach Candy Club where one could enjoy an iced, but non-alcoholic, drink, and have use of a large swimming pool. I could not resist the high diving boards but gave myself a black eye when, while trying to do a somersault, I hit the water face-first having failed to straighten out.

After leaving Bombay we headed back through the Malacca Straits to Dairen in Manchuria. This was our only visit to a communist country (at the time China was in the grip of Mao), and we were treated with quiet distrust but tolerated as a necessary evil while we loaded another grain cargo. An armed guard was permanently stationed on the gangway, and the entire population, apart from the military, appeared to wear a standard uniform of blue overalls, presumably signifying their equality. We were allowed to go ashore but only to walk to a seamen's club and were usually followed. A curfew was placed on us, but the Second Mate and one or two of the engineers managed to find a bar ashore and break the curfew, for which misdemeanor the Captain was severely reprimanded. As this was the nearest we ever got to the China, a country one always thought of as so exotic, I was very disappointed at the drabness of the port and of the life these people seemed to live.

Then we set sail for the long trek back to Europe, passing through the busy Malacca Straits by Singapore again, crossing the Indian Ocean, and heading up the Red Sea, through the Suez Canal and into the Mediterranean. As the world we saw east of Suez was very different from the western hemisphere, being characterised by haze, dust, sand, heat and harsh sun, with distant blue and ochre mountains, but little greenery, it was a relief to be nearing home waters again. While sailors are the most restless people on earth, always anxious to be away at sea when delayed in port, they are always homesick when away and yearn for the civilisation of the West and the green, temperate climate of home.

And so we came to the big port and industrial city of Hamburg, with its bars, bright lights and the notorious Reeperbahn, in a red light district and night club area which was popular with ships' crews but out of bounds to the army personnel stationed in Germany. There, in this large sprawling seaport with its forest of cranes, already regenerating after the devastation of the war, we discharged another cargo of grain. What a contrast from our previous unloading port of Bombay! After that a short hop across the North Sea to Middlesbrough, where the deep-sea crew paid off, and then we were coasting round to Liverpool where the ship was to load her next general cargo, and where I left *Stanhope* to go on leave again.

4

The Sistership Stanburn

MV *Stanburn*. *(Author's ink sketch 1953)*

After a welcome summer leave at home near Farnham, my next appointment in October 1952 was to MV *Stanburn*, the newly delivered sistership of *Stanhope*. Our voyage in this ship was to last more than a year and would encompass Singapore, Malaya, Thailand, Western Australia, India, Pakistan and finally Glasgow. Initially we loaded general cargo in London's Royal Victoria Docks for Singapore, Port Swettenham, Penang and Bangkok. Visiting new foreign ports, particularly in the Far East, was an exciting prospect, though often one could expect little enough time off duty to see more than the immediate vicinity of the dockside. And when one went ashore it was usually alone, as we kept a watch system and colleagues would be on duty.

I was, however, lucky that my parents had friends who had gone to live in Singapore, a kind couple who lived in a comfortable bungalow set on a hillside among the lush green vegetation of the island. They took me to the Raffles Hotel, that bastion of colonial life, and to the Singapore Cricket Club, where I enjoyed the luxury of the swimming pool and tasted the very heavy and dark local Tiger beer. It tended to rain every afternoon, but this didn't interrupt the daily bustle; people walking the streets in their shirtsleeves seemed to steam-dry in that heat in no time. Rickshaws were everywhere and I tried riding in one, but couldn't help but feel sorry for the native lad who expended so much energy in running me along the roads. I also watched a highly entertaining rugby match at the Cricket Club between the local ex-pat team and the Fiji islanders who, playing in their bare feet, were very much the faster and won hands down.

Port Swettenham I remember only for being up a very brown and murky river where lurked many ugly spiky types of fish, but at night the waters were, whenever disturbed, transformed by brilliant purple phosphorescence given off by algae and other minute water creatures. The Malayan people were colourfully clothed but the beauty of many of the young womenfolk was sadly spoiled by the gunmetal-grey teeth fillings they displayed, this being the common form of cheap dentistry at the time.

Penang, by contrast, was an appealingly tidy town with attractive colonial buildings and beautiful parks; I was particularly impressed by seeing a large number of well-groomed schoolchildren in navy-and-white uniforms walking in well-disciplined crocodile formation.

From there to the waters off Bangkok, where any initial disappointment that we were not to go alongside was quickly dispelled by the intriguing nature of the island off which we moored. The ship was there to discharge cargo and we used our own derricks to handle the loads overside into lighters which would then be towed up to Bangkok. This was a leisurely process which took several days as we waited for one barge after another, all of which allowed us plenty of time for looking around. The natives were friendly and would, for a few Woodbines, row us ashore to the nearest island where we could roam at will. Cigarettes, incidentally, were a form of universal currency which we obtained duty free from the 'bond' on board in tins of fifty, either Players or Woodbines.

The nearest island was a tropical dream, which boasted the ruins of a summer palace once used by the kings of Siam, a small Buddhist monastery and a village of straw huts with an opium den. This opium house played the part socially of the village 'local' and I was able to wander in to see a few men lying around on straw mattresses in a haze of sickly sweet smoke.

The island sported giant green lizards and beautiful sandy beaches, with brilliantly clear waters. These waters, while very inviting, were deceptive as they did harbour water snakes and shoals of tiny silver fish. These fish one day attacked me while I was taking a lazy and unsuspecting swim; I felt myself being bitten all over with a thousand pinpricks and I pounded back to the beach faster than I'd ever swum before, though it soon transpired that they had done no lasting harm. I was not after all being devoured by piranhas! Only after I had come out of the water, did I see a water snake, black and about four feet long, wriggling along the shallow foreshore; no more swimming from my tropical island off Bangkok!

At the monastery there were about a dozen orange-robed monks who were keen to show any of us round their peaceful home on a low hill overlooking the sea. In the terraced graveyard they proudly showed me the grave of an English bosun who had suffered a fatal accident when he fell aboard a visiting ship. At the monastery I was given a prayer leaflet beautifully written by hand in an intricate script and illuminated in red and blue dyes on palm fronds. I have it beside me now, more than fifty years later, the blue ink on the yellow parchment-like leaf having faded only slightly.

From there we went to Western Australia to load a series of cargoes of grain for Bombay. We would load in the two small unspoilt ports Geraldton and Bunbury, north and south of Perth respectively. Grain was poured into the holds through shoots from the silos at Geraldton, a delightful harbour, also used by fishermen who particularly targeted crayfish. Somewhat isolated as the port was along the west coast, Geraldton's inhabitants were only too happy to stream on board and couldn't have been more friendly. There was one good hotel where we could enjoy eating the delicious fresh local cray-fish; also a hospital whose nurses provided some much appreciated female company for parties on board, and long sandy beaches with rollers constantly pounding in from the southern Indian Ocean.

A most surprising feature of that most unpretentious small port is the stone-built Roman Catholic Cathedral of St Thomas Xavier on a hill over-looking the harbour. This had been designed by an English architect turned priest, Father John Hawes, who had let his imagination run riot in conceiving this striking cathedral built in the late 1920s. The huge dome covering an octagonal space between nave and chancel is reminiscent of the dome of Florence Cathedral, with similar round windows. There is also a Mexican influence in the design as at the west end of the building are twin towers apparently copied from the Mission of Santa Barbara. Inside the zebra striping of the walls and arches remind one of Siena Cathedral.

At the time, when I went up the hill to Mass at the Cathedral, I had no knowledge of the architect or indeed of his close association with my own family through my grandfather, and of his past influence which was the direct cause for my having been brought up in the Catholic faith.

It is worth digressing from this narrative to say a few words on the architect's life. John Hawes, who later took the name of Fra Jerome, was a most remarkable, talented and holy man and a great friend of my mother's father, Charles Selby-Hall. His life was recorded by Peter F. Anson in his book *The Hermit of Cat Island,* published in 1958 by Burns Oates and dedicated to my grandfather whom Anson befriended while writing that book. Anson, the son of an admiral, himself studied architecture, loved the sea, and was a talented artist and member of the Royal Society of Marine Artists. Like John Hawes he became a monk and wrote many books of nautical and spiritual interest as diverse as *How to Draw Ships* (1941) and T*he Apostleship of the Sea in England and Wales* (1946).

Born in 1876, the son of a devout Protestant solicitor, John Cyril Hawes went to Kings School Canterbury, then studied architecture but, being deeply religious, he became most interested in ecclesiastical architecture and prepared for Anglican orders. Endowed with strong Anglo-Catholic leanings, he determined to model his life on that of St Francis of Assisi. In 1906 he joined the then new Anglican Benedictine community on Caldey Island, combining architectural work with his novitiate. He later travelled to the Bahamas to help with the poor; then on to the United States, where in 1911, he was received into the Roman Catholic Church at about the same time as were the Selby-Halls in England with whom he regularly corresponded. Back in England but still restless, he travelled on a rat-infested emigrant ship *Lake Champlain* to Canada 'running for three days into a field of huge icebergs and dense fog', this in the same year that the *Titanic* sank after striking an iceberg.

Without any available architectural opportunities he worked in Canada as a labourer but returned to England when his mother became ill. With encouragement and financial help from Selby-Hall, he then entered the Beda College in Rome. There, before being ordained into the priesthood at the Lateran Basilica in 1915, he met Bishop Kelly of Geraldton who spoke of the cathedral he wanted built. That October Hawes embarked for Australia where, having duly designed the cathedral and seen it built, he spent a quarter of a century as priest and architect. In 1939 he returned to the Bahamas and settled on Cat Island where he built a small church on a hill with his own hands and lived as a hermit. Several letters home included humorous drawings of the hermitage for his godchild, my sister Jane. It was there on Cat Island that, on his death in June 1956, he was buried in the cave on Mount Alvernia in accordance with his wishes.

To return to the voyage of the *Stanburn*, there came the time to leave Geraldton for the last time with some regrets and goodbyes to girlfriends, but we were finally homeward bound with a cargo of grain. The morning after leaving brought drama when over-consumption of the local 'plonk' caught up with the bosun, a big burly South African, who developed *delirium tremens*; he insisted that 'they' were trying to get him and that we were all in danger, then donned a life jacket and simply stepped overboard. These waters off the Australian coast were a hunting ground for sharks so it was with some trepidation that we turned about and stopped engines to pick him up. The ducking had, however, apparently brought the bosun to his senses for he attempted, rather incongruously, to give orders to the sailors from the water as we lowered a lifeboat for his eventual safe recovery. He was put in the sickbay, where he remained locked up for a few days but was later simply kept under supervision.

During the ensuing weeks until the ship arrived home the bosun placidly accepted his fate and, to occupy himself, embroidered a linen cloth with anchors, the name of our ship and that of our adopted school at Elstead in Surrey, all done with great detail and delicacy. He proudly showed me this very well-executed piece of needlework and our Captain duly sent it to the appreciative school, whose pupils would never be able to imagine how it had come about.

5

The Tanker Stanmore

The tanker *Stanmore*, in which I made a two-year voyage 1954–56.

Having for once been able to take leave at home over Christmas I was promoted to Third Mate, although uncertificated, and sent to join the T2 tanker *Stanmore*, sister to the *Stanwell*, in Amsterdam on the 4th January 1954. Naturally I was delighted to get the promotion, as this involved a huge lift to officer status with decent pay at last and my own cabin. This was, at the age of twenty, six months before the end of my official four-year indentured apprenticeship.

The *Stanmore* was drydocked in Amsterdam for repairs in the most bitterly cold weather imaginable with icicles streaming down the ship's sides. Without any power in drydock, we had only portable heaters to relieve the chill and it was a tremendous relief when, within two weeks, we were off to the sunshine of the Persian Gulf where we loaded a cargo of crude oil for Swansea. Back in Swansea we only stayed long enough to discharge our cargo while paying-off and signing on a new crew, so were away to sea again after just forty-eight hours in a home port. That March my twenty-first birthday was spent uncelebrated as we ploughed our way through the Bay of Biscay heading for the Gulf.

The Third Mate traditionally kept the 8–12 watch on the bridge at sea, being responsible, during those two four-hour watches, for the ship's safe navigation. Apart from avoiding other traffic, this involved seeing that the correct course was kept with regular position fixing by gyro compass bearings when within sight of land; when away from land sun sights would be taken by sextant. The sun sight would be a measurement of the sun's elevation to the nearest minute of angle (i.e. one-sixtieth of a degree) and timed to the nearest second, taken soon after 0800 hours. From this one would calculate a longitudinal position line on the Earth's surface, this being at right angles to the direction of the sun. About four hours later by measuring the maximum altitude at noon, and knowing from daily tables the 'declension' of the sun (i.e. above what latitude within the tropics the sun was vertically positioned), latitude was easily calculated. Then, by judging the course and distance between the two sights, the two position lines, one approximately north/south and the other east/west, were used to fix our position on the chart for noon.

Every watchkeeping officer kept his own sextant and was responsible for correcting it, that is, making minute adjustments to the angles of the mirrors by lining up zero on the Vernier scale with the horizon whenever, through handling or differences in temperature or humidity, this became necessary. I had inherited a very old solid brass sextant from a previous Third Mate on that ship; this had, according to a certificate on the inside lid of the box, first been corrected ashore in Calcutta in 1896. The trouble with this heirloom was that it was very heavy and one of the two mirrors was slightly loose, requiring almost daily adjustment. Regretfully, I did not keep the sextant when I finally left the ship in New York for its antique value would have been – well – astronomical today!

When in port, the Second and Third Mates would divide their duty time, taking turns watch about, as the officer of the watch, tending cargo, moorings, repairs, or taking on water or bunker fuel, and supervising whatever else was going on, while the Chief Officer dealt with the cargo loading schedule, stability calculations, general ship maintenance and the day-to-day running of the ship. It was very important to keep a sharp eye on the mooring lines as they slackened or tightened during loading or discharge as the ship's hull would sink or rise by several feet every hour and the deck watch would have to be called out to tend them. If a wire spring line became too tight it could snap and cause injury.

Having delivered another cargo of crude oil, we paid off back in Swansea on the 5th May; at that time I had almost enough sea time to qualify for sitting my Second Mate's Certificate but the Captain persuaded me to sign on again, after I was allowed to take a few days' leave with my family. This was a decision which I later bitterly regretted, for the next charter to Esso was to keep the ship away for a long hard two-year voyage, whereas I had needed only one more six-week voyage to the Gulf and back to give me the necessary sea time to qualify for sitting my exam.

It was, however, while long and tedious at times, an eventful voyage. That year I witnessed a bit of history while our *Stanmore* was anchored in the River Plate awaiting to discharge a cargo of oil. When we arrived at our anchorage in the river estuary to await orders an armed revolution had just been waged against President Perón. The uprising was supported by the Argentine Navy under Admiral Rochas while Perón was supported by loyal units of the Army. The Navy triumphed; Perón was overthrown and fled to Paraguay, while most of his government fled to Uruguay, taking passage in a Royal Mail Lines passenger ship. Our ship was left out at anchor with many others while the fighting continued, but one morning three Paraguayan frigates steamed past at speed heading out to sea and we were later told that the fleeing Perón had been on board one of these, destined for Spain.

The estuary of the Plate, with Uruguay and its capital Montevideo on the north side and Argentina and its capital Buenos Aires to the south and west, also marks the grave of the German battlecruiser *Graf Spee*, scuttled there early in the Second World War, having been ambushed by British cruisers; one could still see her upper works and topmast breaking the surface.

Under the ship's charter to Esso we endured a seemingly never-ending hard-working six-month stint, during which *Stanmore* was employed as a shuttle tanker transporting crude oil from the rigs in Venezuela's Maracaibo Lake on twelve-hour voyages to the Esso refinery on the island of Aruba in the Dutch West Indies. The wide, shallow and hot sultry Maracaibo Lake was dotted all over with oil rigs, pumps and moorings from which the

As Third Mate aboard *Stanmore*.

condensate could be pumped into lighters and ships. We would moor there at pontoons for about eight hours at a time without ever getting close to shore, our cargo manifold being connected to pipelines which were lifted from the lake under the pontoons. We could only load a part cargo because there was limited water depth and hence a draught restriction at the bar. Having made passage through the narrow channel over the bar leading out to sea, we would, about ten hours later, dock at the smoke-belching Esso refinery in Aruba, discharge our cargo and return immediately to the lake. This cycle would be repeated about every forty-eight hours. The Second Mate and I were obliged to work watch about, whether at sea or working cargo in port, while we both had to turn out to assist with mooring each time we docked or cast off, so we found ourselves working about 14 hours a day in the tropical heat without ever a day off for weeks on end.

The monotony was, however, suddenly and dramatically relieved when, on crossing the bar with our maximum load one day, we struck bottom for a moment due to an unusually high swell. The ship shuddered briefly under the impact before we carried on our way. However, the Lloyd's Surveyor, called in to inspect the hull at Aruba, detected a cracked keelplate right aft and, to the delight of the crew, prescribed drydocking for repairs, though the charterers, shipping company and insurers would not have been so happy. After discharging our cargo at Aruba we made our hull temporarily watertight in the traditional manner taught in seamanship manuals by building a cement box over the damaged plate. To do this one simply knocks together a rough wooden box around the damaged area, the box being shored from the nearest frames and beams, and then fills the box space with cement. To the joy of the whole crew the nearest suitable drydock for repairing the keelplate was considered to be New York, so there we made our way shortly before Christmas.

At first sight the Manhattan skyline and Statue of Liberty are always breathtaking but it was especially welcome to us after so long away from civilisation. The ship was docked at a repair yard in Brooklyn for three weeks and, in stark contrast to the tropical heat of Venezuela, during a spell of bitterly cold weather. We had only temporary heating arrangements for, without available cooling water, the ship's generators were shut down. But this didn't bother us and there was plenty of time to go ashore and explore Manhattan, Central Park and Broadway. I did all the obvious things when off duty: I went to Radio City to see Bing Crosby in *White Christmas*, watched skating in Rockefeller Plaza, visited St Patrick's Cathedral, took the lift up to the top of the Empire State Building, ate a vast helping of blueberry pie at a bar counter, was amazed to be asked if I were over eighteen at a bar (for now I was a weathered sailor of five years), shook hands with the previous world heavyweight boxing champion, Jack Dempsey, at his popular restaurant on Broadway, and saw a memorable Broadway play, *The Lark*, with Julie Harris playing St Joan.

With *Stanmore* back in service, one of our most interesting passages during that two-year voyage took us to a small oil loading berth at Carapito a day and a night's journey up the winding Orinoco River in Venezuela. With dense jungle on either side the *Stanmore* was guided up the narrow upper reaches by a local pilot with intimate knowledge of the river; navigation marks were few and far between so at night he directed the darkened ship by moonlight. When it came time to turn the ship round, because there was not the width to turn a ship of more than 400 feet length conventionally in the river, the pilot drove the ship's bow into the soft mud of the bank and used the engine with helm hard over to swing the stern round. Since it is every seaman's instinct to avoid going aground, our Captain, who had not been forewarned, was somewhat alarmed by this procedure, as was the Chief Officer standing at 'anchor stations' on the forecastle as he and the bow disappeared briefly into the dense undergrowth. However, all was well and, as the stern swung round, we slid smoothly out.

Another strange adventure saw us moored at an oil jetty near Palambang, Sumatra. When it came time to leave a large proportion of the crew had not returned aboard; they were obviously enjoying the hospitality of the local villagers, particularly the local brew and the womenfolk. The Captain decided to send me to round the crew up and I was promptly handed the agent's bicycle and went on my way to do the rounds of the local huts. It was not a simple task to knock on the doors of primitive straw huts but when various noises suggested that there were sailors within I had to tell them that their time was up. Although reluctant to return, the sailors were eventually persuaded to do so.

One of the most dramatic incidents aboard *Stanmore* was the day we were overtaken by a typhoon while moored in the Japanese harbour of Osaka waiting to discharge cargo. The harbour has a huge basin pretty well surrounded by breakwaters; within this haven, oceangoing ships lay at mooring buoys and there were a great many smaller ships and boats alongside as well. Shortly after 0600, when I had just come on deck to relieve the Second Mate who'd kept the night watch, a harbour launch sped alongside; an official shouted up to warn us that a typhoon was approaching from the south and would probably be with us by midday. The launch then hurried on to pass its message to the next ship. I woke the Captain who didn't seem greatly concerned. However, when the Chief Officer turned out at 0700 with the bosun and dayworkers, the barometer was already dropping fast and the wind increasing, so they set about putting out extra mooring wires over the bow to the huge mooring buoy at which the ship swung. Meanwhile there was a bustle of activity on other ships around; some carried anchor cables out to their buoys while some, including the Blue Funnel cargo liner next to us, steamed out to sea in order to ride out the coming storm more safely in open water. All this time, under a grey sky of scudding clouds, the wind began to howl and the rain to drive across the sea surface, but we were protected from the worst of the heavy seas by the rocky breakwater piles over which the waves were now breaking in a continuous barrage.

It was fortunate that we were prepared just in time, for Typhoon Marie struck us with its full force by 0930, three hours earlier than originally forecast. What impressed me most was how, accompanied by an almighty roar of wind, the rain, blown spume, sky and sea formed one indistinguishable grey blanket of wet noise. We could no longer venture on deck but I stood in one of the more sheltered alleyway doors watching in awe as, in a single blast, the Red Ensign flying from the mainmast was shredded to bits, halyards blowing out horizontally. Meanwhile the engine room was manned and on standby to give manoeuvring power when necessary as the Captain anxiously watched our wire moorings surging between the bow hawse pipes and the buoy while the ship yawed about as though demented. We were lucky that we held. Others were not so lucky; one smaller ship, flying the flag of Nationalist China and the code flag X for 'I require assistance' drifted past us within a few metres as she dragged her anchors shorewards. The local newspaper reported afterwards that altogether 200 ships, small craft and boats had been wrecked or damaged. Two hours after striking us, Typhoon Marie had sped on northwards, but was tragically to sink a ferry with one thousand people on board after passing to the north side of the island.

Shipping lanes in the open sea were always busy with tankers and frequently it was necessary to take evasive action, particularly when the busiest lanes crossed one another. The golden rule was to watch the compass bearing of an approaching ship and if this didn't change then one was on a collision course. The Rule of the Road, or 'Articles' – all the pages of which incidentally we had to learn by heart for our Second Mate's ticket – specified that when two vessels were crossing, the one which had the other on the starboard side should give way while the other should stand on.

There was one occasion, however, when a fully loaded tanker approached from our port side to cross our course; it was his responsibility to give way and, clearly not having kept a proper watch out, he left this too late so that in turning to starboard he turned too close towards us. The Captain beside me jumped up and down, shouting, 'He's going to hit us!' and for all the world it looked as though this lumbering giant would. The other ship's bow swung to starboard until it was pointing directly towards our bridge, then just paid off in time to pass within a few feet under our stern; a very near miss for two ships each of several hundred feet in length, the other loaded with fuel oil, and ourselves with dangerous gas-filled tanks. Having just discharged our cargo, the ship was in that most explosive state of having a mixture of oil fumes and air in the tanks, and if the two ships had collided the whole world, ourselves excepted, would have known about it!

After discharging each cargo, we always started tank cleaning when out at sea and then ventilated the tanks to make them 'gas free' before visiting our next port. In those days we would pump the oily mixture overboard from each tank when out of territorial waters, a procedure since strictly forbidden, special tanks nowadays being fitted in the cargo spaces to take the slops for later discharge ashore.

As the months passed, it became increasingly obvious that the charterers had no intention of bringing our ship back to the UK, so we had to stay on board the full two-year term without ever a day's leave. Morale was low and this led to a certain amount of drunken discontent among the crew when in port. At sea there was nothing but our routine work to occupy us

– off duty we would read books from the ship's library or listen to the radio.

One sailor did manage to get sent home early. Coming back from ashore the worse for drink while the ship was discharging cargo in Aruba, he stepped off the gangway onto the cargo deck, lit a match and threw it towards the open lids of the cargo tanks. Under the right conditions this could have caused an almighty explosion, so, as officer of the watch, I had no alternative but to call the dock police and he was locked up for the night. The offending seaman was paid off and eventually sent home as a 'Distressed British Seaman', the title under which, by arrangement with the local consul, crew members who have had to be discharged abroad are shipped back to the UK on the next suitable British-flag ship.

The rest of us were finally discharged in New York on 13th March 1956, my twenty-third birthday, then flown home in an old DC3 aircraft chartered from Icelandic Airways. This was the first time I had ever flown and it was indeed memorable. It turned out that the cabin crew had never flown the Atlantic before. Owing to a leaking fuel line smoking was forbidden and it was suggested that we should wrap up well overnight because there was no heating in the cabin and the temperature was 40 below outside. Finally, the following midday, we descended through a blanket of low cloud to Heathrow, there to be united with our families. Our seemingly interminable voyage in the tanker *Stanmore* was over at last, and I resolved never to go to sea in another tanker.

6

Taking the Second Mate's Ticket

Back home I went to study for my Second Mate's Certificate at the King Edward VII Nautical College in the East End of London along with other cadets from a whole range of tanker, cargo and passenger shipping companies. This college is in Limehouse close to the London Docklands and those of us from outside London were conveniently accommodated at a seaman's hostel opposite, generally known as the 'Stack of Bricks'; possibly not the most salubrious place to spend one's first summer months at home after years away but practical. While studying we were required to queue up each week to collect dole money from the local labour exchange, although according to the rules the balance of our pay was made up for three months by the companies for which we had been working.

I attended King Edward VII for the early summer term, each course being structured to last for twelve weeks, though there was nothing to stop one doing a second term if one failed any part of the exams. These exams were split into three – written, oral and signals – and one had to pass all three to acquire one's ticket. The written exams comprised coastal and celestial navigation, involving spherical trigonometry; meteorology, including knowledge of the characteristics of typhoons and hurricanes; basic ship construction and stability; and cargo work with knowledge of the more dangerous cargoes. Dry cargoes of specific significance included coal, which gives off dangerously explosive gas; grain, which needs to be fed into the sides and corners of holds, usually by hand from a hatchway feeder constructed each time from wood dunnage; timber on deck, which absorbs moisture and affects stability; and sulphur, which is susceptible to spontaneous combustion.

The orals, before a Board of Trade examiner who was himself an ex-ship's master, were the most nerve-racking, and the examiners could be quite intimidating. The exam included seamanship and the theory of ship handling, particularly mooring and anchoring procedures with the aid of models. Some of the seamanship in the curriculum was quite archaic, including such operations as rigging sea anchors, making way under jury sails if the engine failed and rigging a jury rudder if broken down, or passing a canvas tarpaulin under the hull to block a leak – fine in theory but hardly practical in oceangoing-sized ships. The main focus, however, was on instilling into us the 'Rule of the Road at Sea', which in practice required us to learn by heart and be able to quote from any of the 'Articles', which, though swathed in long-winded legal language, were simply the rules relating to how sailing vessels, fishing vessels or ships under power should give way to one another, whether crossing, meeting end on, overtaking or obstructed in any way, and the lights and signals to be carried by these vessels underway and at anchor.

Signals exams included tests in Morse code, both audio and visual, as well as semaphore using hand-carried flags. Morse was important as it was in general use at the time in order to communicate by signal lamp with other ships or shore stations; the officer on the bridge would do this with the battery-operated Aldis lamp, which gave a beam of light triggered to focus on the target by a reflecting mirror. This was before VHF or other radio telephone systems were in use. Regular Morse radio signalling was the domain of the radio operator of which each cargo vessel carried just one, who worked certain watch times. Semaphore had long since gone out of use in practice, but our curriculum still required us to learn it for exam purposes.

One other exam required was for the St John's Ambulance First Aid Certificate. This required us only to attend a series of lectures outside normal study times, and we passed automatically on paying the examining doctor 10 shillings. I'm afraid that, being preoccupied with our other exams, none of us paid this subject the attention which it really deserved, a point which I didn't fully appreciate until I later found myself in charge of the ship's medicine chest while being required, as a Second Mate in Royal Mail cargo vessels, to act as 'ship's doctor', which could be quite a nerve-racking responsibility.

To my great relief I passed all my Second Mate's exams at the first attempt and so was able to take a much appreciated period of summer leave with my parents while I considered which shipping company to choose for my future career. I had already had my fill of tankers so I wanted to join a fleet that included none of these; this ruled out one company for which I had great respect, namely the Royal Fleet Auxiliary (RFA), whose naval supply ships included a large proportion of tankers, although I did meet several lads who enjoyed working for the RFA. This company, under the Blue Ensign, supplied the fleet and bunkering ports of the Royal Navy from ships stationed in such strategic ports as Malta or Gibraltar, where the officers were able to join in the social life of the Royal Navy. Although RFA ships engaged in complicated manoeuvres with RN ships, including refuelling them while underway at sea, they were manned by merchant service personnel and run as merchant ships, thereby having the economic advantage of employing far smaller crews than RN ships.

My aim then was to chose, and hopefully be accepted by, a shipping line of mixed cargo and regular passenger ships, on voyages of not more than three or four months; in that way life at sea would be far more interesting than the monotonous routine offered by tankers or bulk carriers. With more frequent periods of leave, I would also be able to have a more regular home life without feeling like a stranger among my family, friends and neighbours each time I came home. So I looked out for a company with just these attributes that might have vacancies for deck officers.

Plans by Royal Mail Lines to have built, at Harland & Wolff in Belfast, three new passenger–cargo liners of a unique design for the South American service, first caught my eye when publicised in the newspapers while I was home on leave that summer of 1956. Royal Mail Lines also ran some smaller cargo ships up and down the Brazilian and Argentine coast bringing home timber from the Brazilian forests, as well as general cargo, bales of cotton and sugar from Central American ports and the Caribbean. There were in addition some rather smarter and newer cargo liners carrying up to twelve passengers each, these transporting general cargo to the West Indies and through Panama to the Pacific coast of America. Their terminal port was Vancouver, where they turned for home, loading with timber and fruit, the latter in cool chambers, from ports including Victoria and New Westminster in British Columbia, and further citrus fruit along with general cargo from Californian ports such as Los Angeles and San Francisco, and thence back to the UK and Europe, so making round voyages of about three months. It was not surprising therefore that the Royal Mail fleet and its various itineraries appealed to me.

Walking back and forward,
Watching to the Westward,
Waiting for the sunset,
The twilight follows on,
Golden clouds are darting,
Daylight now departing,
Hush the breeze of evening
As the darkness closes in.

Navigator standing,
Hand with sextant holding,
Waiting for the evening stars
To light their silver lamps.
Antares, Altair, Spica,
Arcturus and Vega;
Find him out and fix him
On the South Atlantic chart.

Eight bells now are striking,
The first watch comes, relieving,
The course is handed over
That cleaves the path for home.
Homing to the Northward,
Homing North and Eastward,
Steaming to Southampton
Where the big ships lie.

From RMS *Andes' Dolphin* magazine, August 1953

7

To Sea with Royal Mail Lines

It is a privilege to have served with Royal Mail Lines (RML), which, in an earlier life as the Royal Mail Steam Packet Co., had played such a pioneering role in the development of steamship services around the world and of the very fabric of the British Merchant Navy. I have outlined, in an Appendix to this volume, the origins and very eventful history of this company, which spanned more than 120 years and played its part in all the major British and world conflicts. But in that summer of 1956 I was looking to my future and thinking of the new cargo–passenger liners which had just been ordered by RML for the South American service. The company now served the west coast of North America as well as the West Indies and the east coast of South America, including Rio de Janeiro, Santos, Montevideo and Buenos Aires. By regularly carrying all classes of passengers, from Anglo-Argentine landowners to Spanish and Portuguese emigrants, from diplomatic staff and businessmen to schoolchildren, as well as general cargo, machinery, mail and bullion, RML had played a leading role in establishing the railways, businesses and estancias in Brazil and Argentina. The company was also a significant player in the meat trade as its ships brought thousands of tons of chilled and frozen beef back to London on each voyage, a service which had been crucial to feeding the UK during the war years.

I applied to Royal Mail and was duly interviewed at Royal Mail House in Leadenhall Street, an imposing edifice built in the best traditions of the City and London's shipping communities. One entered the portals through a marble arch to see awe-inspiring ship models, a war memorial plaque and the bell of the old *Almanzora*, a passenger ship which had survived both major wars. A high-ceilinged main hall housed the positively Dickensian outward and homeward freight departments, and tucked away up an old-fashioned lift on the mezzanine floor were the personnel department and marine superintendent's office where I was interviewed.

43

There were vacancies as not all those cadets who had served their time at sea with Royal Mail necessarily stayed with the same company. I was immediately given an initial two-year contract and my seniority or ranking in the RML 'Bluebook' began from that date. This Bluebook listing became all important with Royal Mail's career officers in their later years as, provided copybooks were not blotted, it governed future promotions, even right up to a senior captain's final appointment as Commodore of the Fleet.

So, in October 1956, in a brief initiation to the company, I made a short coastal trip with a relief crew from Liverpool to London as Fourth Mate in the 10,000-grt *Loch Ryan*. Previously the 1943-built steamer *Empire Chieftain*, one of a dozen Government ships which had been managed by Royal Mail through the war years, *Loch Ryan* had been purchased in 1946 by RML for the North Pacific trade. She was 2–3 knots faster than the average wartime cargo ship; the extra speed of the 15-knot turbine-powered *Loch Ryan,* built by Furness Shipbuilding, had been incorporated into the design as a counter to submarine attack. Decks, holds and lifting gear were all designed for carrying goods of unusual size and weight.

Then on 24th October I was appointed Fourth Officer of the fine-looking 11,000-grt RMS *Loch Gowan* for my first deep-sea voyage with the company. Built at Harland & Wolff, Belfast, just two years previously in 1954, *Loch Gowan* was a twin-deck cargo ship with five holds and a 30-ton heavy lift derrick housed at the foot of the mainmast. This was a fairly standard cargo-handling arrangement for that time. The Harland & Wolff steam turbine propulsion engine, with double reduction gear, drove a single-screw propeller to give speeds of up to 16 knots. She was engaged with three other Royal Mail vessels, *Loch Ryan* and the sisters, *Loch Garth* and *Loch Avon*, on a joint service with Holland America Line voyaging between northern Europe and North Pacific ports.

Loch Gowan sailed out of the Royal Victoria Docks, London for Bermuda, Kingston Jamaica, Cristobal, then through the Panama Canal, to Los Angeles, San Francisco, Seattle, Victoria and Vancouver, returning via the same ports to Liverpool and London. The ship had accommodation for up to twelve passengers who might travel between any of the ports but, for the sum of £400, passengers could enjoy the full round voyage cruise. This fair-weather voyage, with stopovers in each port, comfortable accommodation and the luxury of a tiled swimming pool and good food, made this a very popular trip for passengers.

As Fourth Officer on the North Pacific run, I was on the 4–8 watch under the Chief Officer while at sea, and assisted the Third Officer on cargo watches in port. The Master of a ship was always considered almighty, and I remember the *Loch Gowan* particularly for our very strict and some-time heavy-drinking Captain, who had little patience with green junior officers like myself. On one or two occasions, he would come up to the bridge and give erratic orders to the helmsman to turn the ship about, or to the officer of the watch to man the lifeboats. Our Chief Officer was, however, skilful at dealing with these alarming bouts. I've no doubt the Captain's behaviour was connected in his mind with harrowing wartime experiences, but there was certainly a propensity among some ships' masters, who had a lonely enough job in command, to overindulge in alcohol. Merchant ships were far from dry at sea and liquor was always cheap and easily obtained by those on board. For all that, masters who had spent a lifetime at sea were generally deeply respected, and several, with exemplary war records, had been deservedly decorated.

Paying off in Liverpool next February for leave between voyages of the *Loch Gowan*, I was at last able to try my hand at a winter skiing holiday, and I became absolutely hooked. After that I went skiing every year that I had the opportunity to take winter leave. Joining an Inghams holiday to Westendorf in the Tyrol that first time, I was entranced by the atmosphere of this beautiful farming village deep in snow. I enjoyed the challenge and fun of my first week on the nursery slopes followed by more adventurous trips up the only local ski lift in that unspoilt village, all under the tutorage of local ski instructors. It was a thrill just to get a bronze medal from the ski school in a race at the end of the fortnight.

The following year I was able to go to Alpbach, one of the most pictur-esque small Tyrolean villages offering traditional after-ski Tyrolean music and dancing in the two local inns. Then one Christmas I spent in Obergurgl high up a valley at some 7,000 feet; there it was very icy but it was an unforgettable experience to attend Midnight Mass on a cold crisp night in a fairy-tale setting with the local choirboys singing 'Silent Night'.

Thereafter I had scope for more adventurous skiing in the fairly quiet Italian Alpine villages of Macunaga and Madesimo and some more popular resorts, as well as for traditional skiing in Switzerland, which had been the original home of British winter sports. I took one holiday at the Swiss village of Grindlewald which offered dramatic views of the Jungfrau Glacier. I found magic both in the quiet isolation when gliding alone through the pine trees with large flakes of snow drifting silently down around, and in exhil-arating hard-packed runs under bright blue skies. Grindlewald, one of the oldest skiing resorts, was the very place where my mother and father had first met in the 1920s; she with a group from Cambridge and he with a group from Oxford University.

Then there was the more concentrated skiing in purpose-built French resorts such as those in the Trois Vallées which boasted wonderful long open runs above the treeline. In later years while working in London I would occasionally go for weekend skiing to Scotland, taking a bus from Hendon or by train to Inverness, but that was pretty hard work and each time I promised myself not to go again. The conditions were usually hairy; rain, sleet, snow and gales were the order of the day with rocks, heather, mud and puddles ready to trap one on the lower slopes. To be going up to the summit of Glencoe on a chairlift while soaked through by driving sleet was not much fun. Just once I went for a four-day early May bank holiday to Cairngorm and experienced the bliss of blue skies and deep fresh snow.

I took my final skiing holiday abroad more than twenty-five years after my first visit to the nursery slopes of Westendorf, this last time staying in the Italian village of Cormayeur on the French border under the shadow of Mont Blanc. The climax to my Alpine skiing adventures was, after ascending by cable car, to ski down Mont Blanc to Chamonix in a small party. There was, of course, a guide, something about which the French authorities were very strict – they would refuse to rescue anyone skiing down without an official guide. There were a great many crevasses in the blue ice to be negotiated, so, in fact, we had only short uninterrupted runs during the steep descent and in places it was more of a downward climb on skis with some spectacular but frightening views through walls of snow and ice of the valleys below.

After two voyages with *Loch Gowan* I was appointed Third Officer of the 6,950-grt *Brittany* where we made one particularly memorable voyage down to South America. One of the smaller, less pretentious motor cargo ships, but a very happy one under Captain Allason-Jones, *Brittany* had been built by William Pickersgill & Sons of Sunderland in 1946, and was powered by a 3,340-bhp 6-cylinder diesel engine giving her a speed of 12 knots. *Brittany* took the place of a namesake lost during the war, the latter having done sterling work ferrying refugees out of Singapore as the colony fell to the Japanese.

Among the general cargo we loaded for Brazil aboard *Brittany* in Liverpool were a number of railway bogeys, those heavy wheel sections of carriages, weighing some 7 tons each. They had been secured by wire lashings in No.2 hold just forward of the bridge, but in the very heavy Atlantic weather we experienced on that outward voyage, two bogeys broke loose and careered across the hold with each violent roll, thus sounding the most alarming rumbling noise throughout the ship. We reduced speed and hove to, but there was no way we could secure these dangerous beasts until the weather had eased. There was a real danger that they could crack open the ship's hull plates. However, having caused utter carnage among the other cargo, the bogeys ended up firmly embedded in now badly mangled sacks of cement which had, fortuitously, been stowed in the same hold.

Homeward bound from Porto Alegre in Brazil we carried a more secure cargo of timber in the holds and on deck. Timber cargoes do have one idiosyncratic characteristic. Timber being stacked as high on deck as initial stability and the view from the bridge will allow means that the ship's centre of gravity (CG) is correspondingly high, but when deck timber absorbs moisture the CG becomes even higher; the ship is then liable to list several degrees to port or starboard, taking up an 'angle of loll' at which the CG adjusts to line up vertically with the centre of buoyancy of the cross section of the submerged hull in its listed state; this is, however, not generally a critical condition with timber, and it was quite common to see a timber-loaded ship steaming along at an apparently alarming angle of heel.

Returning to Liverpool in October 1957, I had acquired sufficient sea time to go up for my First Mate's Certificate, for which I duly went to study at Sir John Cass College in London, staying, rather comfortably, in the Merchant Navy Hotel at Lancaster Gate and commuting daily to Aldgate. Going up for one's 'ticket' involved concentrated hard work if one was to pass the exams at term end, although it was, as with the Second Mate's exam, possible to stay on for a further term if necessary. A few officers, particularly after long sea voyages and little leave, took advantage of the shoreside break to linger for two or three terms. But all the students enjoyed their study break, not least because it gave an opportunity to meet and share experiences with contemporaries of similar ranking from widely different shipping companies, who might have sailed to every corner of the globe, whether in passenger liner, cargo liner, tanker, tramp ship, even cable layers and fleet support ships.

As a result of yarning in the local pubs, and consumption of a great deal of beer of an evening, those more envious of others might, depending on their contractual obligations, be tempted to switch allegiance to another company. However, there tended on the whole to be a strong competitive spirit and pride among the officers of different companies with loyalty to their own.

Thus we again studied seamanship, cargo work, navigation, ship handling, meteorology and signalling though to a somewhat higher standard than for Second Mate, and with the addition of ship's business studies. Being qualified to sail as First Mate meant having to be capable in particular of dealing with ship discipline, the stability of the ship and distribution of cargo, the upkeep and daily maintenance of the entire ship and accommodation, barring the engine room and electrical installations, which were the Chief Engineer's domain, and also of taking over the Master's duties at sea in emergency.

Contemporary postcard of *Highland Monarch* (c 1950).

Having passed my exams after a three-month term of cramming and after taking some leave at home with my parents, I joined one of the most interesting ships in the Royal Mail fleet, *Highland Monarch*, in April 1958. She was one of a unique series of six twin-funnelled passenger cargo ships built by Harland & Wolff between 1929 and 1932, originally for the Nelson Line, which was later absorbed by Royal Mail. One of these sisterships, the *Highland Patriot*, was a replacement for the *Highland Hope*, previously wrecked while under Nelson Line colours. The *Patriot*, however, was to be an early casualty of the Second World War. She was dogged by U-boats and took evading action by taking zigzagging courses on her Atlantic crossings. Initially she survived a U-boat attack in January 1940 in the South Atlantic; reportedly, five torpedoes were fired at her and all missed, whereupon the *Patriot* opened fire with her light gun and with remarkable luck damaged the U-boat, driving it off. In May that year she was stranded, fully laden, in the Thames estuary, a sitting duck for German bombers, but RAF fighters kept watch over the helpless vessel for two days while a cargo of tomatoes was discharged and she was refloated by tugs. Then her luck ran out: homeward bound from South America with cargo and some forty passengers, some of whom were about to enlist, the *Highland Patriot* was torpedoed and sunk by a U-boat 500 miles off the Wolf Rock. Of some 150 persons on board only the lives of three engineers were lost. The ensuing fire, which burnt for several hours – there was so much wood used in the internal panelling of these ships that fire was always a risk – gave sufficient light to enable the crew to abandon ship in good order. A patrolling British warship HMS *Wellington*, seeing smoke on the horizon, set course for the sinking ship and rescued all the survivors from their well-ordered convoy of lifeboats.

Thus there were left four *Highland* boats, *Princess, Chieftain, Brigade* and *Monarch*, plying a regular service to South America and bringing much needed foodstuffs to Britain. Meanwhile it appears that *Highland Monarch* may have unknowingly provided the bait that allowed the German battleship *Graf Spee* to be trapped and sunk in the River Plate by ships of the British South Atlantic Force. According to one of the captured merchant skippers who had been held in the German battleship, there was on board a copy of the *Buenos Aires Herald*, the English-speaking daily, giving a list of shipping departures from Buenos Aires which included a mention of *Highland Monarch*. Captain Langsdorf's ambition to sink that liner was thought to have influenced his decision to head for the River Plate, where the Royal Navy closed in on her.

The *Highland*s were all soon requisitioned for troop transports. Their terminal port was switched to Liverpool, this being less vulnerable than the London Docks and they voyaged as far afield as Australia and New Zealand. Hostilities over, in early 1946, the *Highland Monarch* was given the special task of repatriating those of the 320 surviving crew of the battleship *Graf Spee* who had been interned throughout the war and wished to return to Germany. All four *Highland* ships survived the war and were re-engaged by Royal Mail on a regular ten-week round voyage to South America. As the *Highland* boats, now some thirty years old, were coming to the end of their lives, I was grateful to have had the fascinating experience of a making a round voyage to Buenos Aires in the *Highland Monarch*, and, incidentally, passing again the wreck of the *Graf Spee* in the estuary of the River Plate.

The four *Highland*s carried general cargo and passengers in different classes: 150 first class, 70 intermediate class and 500 third class, the latter including Spanish and Portuguese emigrants outward bound from Vigo and Lisbon to Rio de Janeiro and Buenos Aires respectively. Homeward bound the ships would carry thousands of tons of frozen and chilled meat, a cargo which was regularly discharged in London's Royal Victoria Docks, mainly for distribution through Smithfield Market. The Argentine chilled beef had to be delivered to the shops within three weeks of loading direct from the *frigorificos* on the banks of the River Plate at Buenos Aires and La Plata. This meat trade was the key to Royal Mail's profitability.

Highland Monarch completes her last voyage before going to the breakers from London's Royal Victoria Dock, 1960. *(Author's photo)*

The *Highland*s were unique in appearance with a long weather deck, passenger accommodation block amidships, topped by two squat flat-topped raked funnels. A separate smaller block of bridge accommodation, including deck officers' and Captain's quarters, was set well forward of the main block. The space between the two main accommodation blocks, which, unusually, extended right down to the weather deck, allowed cranes to swing over the deck between to plumb the centre cargo hold (No.3) when working cargo.

With double-acting four-cycle twin-screw diesel propulsion and a speed requirement of 16 knots, these ships could, in addition to the passengers, carry baggage, mail, cars and general or refrigerated cargo in five holds.

The public rooms of the *Highland Monarch*'s first-class passenger accommodation were remarkably fitted out, having an oak-panelled saloon/library with lead-paned windows in the style of a baronial hall, while the Tudor-style dining room with internal bay windows had Welsh dressers laden with securely fixed willow-pattern china. Furthermore, the teak-sheathed boat deck was marked out forward of the twin funnels not only for deck quoits but also with a cricket pitch. Boundary circles indicated the number of runs scored by any hit, while nets could be erected around the perimeter to catch the boundary balls before they disappeared into the Atlantic.

At sea, when the ship approached the tropics, a swimming pool of wood and canvas would be rigged up over No.3 hatch. Another extraordinary feature was that, outward bound, temporary accommodation bulkheads were rigged to carry emigrants in the upper (or shelter) decks of Nos. 4 and 5 holds, not the most luxurious of accommodation, and in stark contrast to the old-world luxury of first class. On arrival at Buenos Aires, the temporary bulkheads would be dismantled and the same spaces hosed down, cooled and prepared for slinging carcasses of chilled beef from meat hooks.

The *Highland* boats, with their modest size and intimate atmosphere, were very popular with regular passengers sailing to and from South America and had a reputation for providing excellent cuisine, which would of course always include the best South American beef steaks. Certainly they provided the most enjoyable way of travelling to and from Brazil and Argentina and had carried more than half a million passengers by the time they came out of service, the last to arrive back in London being the *Highland Monarch* in April 1960. She then went ignominiously to the British Iron & Steel Corporation on the Clyde for breaking up, so ending a unique era of passenger and cargo traffic to South America.

Their successors, the three new 20,348-ton A-boats *Amazon*, *Aragon* and *Arlanza*, were now being built at Harland & Wolff under a $60-million contract in 1959–60, the last ships built for Royal Mail Lines and the last ever ships to feature separate accommodation for first, second and third-class passengers. With twin turbo-diesel engines they would make 17.5 knots and carry 449 passengers along with general cargo in five holds, mail lockers and bullion rooms. Homeward bound they would, like the *Highland*s before them, bring some 4,500 tons of chilled and frozen meat from Argentina and Uruguay.

Meanwhile, having left the *Monarch*, I was re-appointed in August 1958 to the west coast of North America service, this time as Third Officer in the *Loch Garth* for two voyages and then to the newly built 11,000-ton *Loch Loyal*, sister to *Loch Gowan*, and another very comfortable ship for passengers and crew.

RMS *Loch Garth* entering the Panama Canal locks. *(Author's photo 1958)*

I made six voyages as Third Mate to the North Pacific over the next three years. This was a very pleasant and colourful route mainly blessed with fair weather. It involved calling at Bermuda overnight, with perhaps an opportunity for a short run ashore, then to Kingston, Jamaica for two days, a bit of a shantytown always full of life, noise and bustle; and from there onwards to the Panama Canal. One spent a full day negotiating the Canal under the control of an American pilot, with the ship guided through each lock by a series of 'mules'. A mule is a type of electric tram with a winch holding a tensioned mooring wire secured to bitts (or mooring bollards) at the ship's bow or stern.

After clearing the Canal we generally had a clear week's run up the Pacific coast in beautiful weather with distant views of the Mexican mountains, often visible at more than 60 miles, and a voyage notable for glorious sunrises and sunsets, before approaching Los Angeles. During this passage the ship's swimming pool would be in full use by the passengers and, at certain hours, the officers and crew were also permitted to use it. While the *Gowan* and *Loyal* each had a built-in tiled swimming pool on a raised deck forward of the bridge, the older ships like *Loch Garth* also had a pool, but one which could be erected on the foredeck out of wood and canvas and was just sufficient to splash around in during hot weather. This type of pool could, however, get damaged by heavy seas in bad weather, so sometimes had to be hastily dismantled.

The port for Los Angeles was Wilmington, which mainly comprised a series of long concrete warehouses set in a flat and rather arid landscape. The ship's officers and crew rarely had time to visit the city of Los Angeles; instead, while working cargo, we would listen out for the gong of the 'Good Humor' man coming along the quay with his trolley of ice creams, often our only contact with the shore. I did once go to nearby Long Beach

Swimming pool erected on *Loch Garth*'s foredeck for passengers and crew. *(Author's photo 1958)*

where the most notable feature was the three-funnelled *Queen Mary*, newly anchored off the beach. Previously the pride of the Cunard Line and winner of the Blue Riband for the fastest crossing of the Atlantic in pre-war days, and now bought by a US consortium, she was moored, majestically but rather incongruously, offshore, waiting to be turned into a tourist attraction.

Our next stop would be San Francisco. This port always gave one a lift from the time one approached, among a myriad of pleasure boats, passing under the Golden Gate suspension bridge. We would tie up right on Fisherman's Wharf, where we could look down from the ship's deck on a line of fish restaurants. These were just beginning to become trendy, and the mouthwatering aroma of shellfish wafting up to the forecastle as we secured the mooring lines, encouraged us to get everything tied down and ourselves ashore for our supper as quickly as possible. Certainly we enjoyed the local fare enormously. A walk ashore, through China Town and up Nob Hill, was always worthwhile, with its magnificent views of the bay including the convict island of Alcatraz, as were the legendary tram rides. Although San Francisco enjoys a very pleasant sunny climate, it is famous for its fogs, caused by the contrasts of the cool sea currents and dry Californian desert air. Dense fog would roll across the bay without warning, obscuring everything, including the bridge, although not necessarily to a great height so that the topmasts of ships and the towers of the bridge would often remain visible while we could see only a few yards ahead of us at water level. Through this blanket of fog there would sound a cacophony of whistles, horns and

RMS *Loch Loyal* at Los Angeles 1959.

sirens, from the largest ships to the smallest boats, echoing around the bay; dangerous conditions to be caught in when underway.

From San Francisco we had a two-day voyage up the west coast to Seattle, and sometimes also upriver to Portland, where the landscape gives way to hills and pine trees with distant views of snowcapped mountains.

The main responsibility of a Third Mate in Royal Mail, apart from keeping the 8–12 watch at sea, was that of cargo officer. As such he was responsible for overseeing the stevedoring on board, recording where all cargo was loaded, seeing that it was all discharged in the right ports, and drawing up the detailed cargo plans during the voyage showing where every parcel of cargo was stowed on each deck in the five holds and on deck. This job reached its climax on completion of the homeward bound loading schedule in the terminal port of Vancouver. Before sailing, a complete cargo plan on a 3ft long ship's profile drawing had to be filled in by hand. This was done using chinagraph colour pencils showing the quantity, identification and destination of each batch of cargo. This sheet was pressed on to a flat jelly tray and some thirty copies were then taken from this for distribution to the shipping company and for forwarding to agents who would be responsible for engaging stevedores at each discharging port, as well as for use on board. Very often this job, carried out jointly by the Third and Fourth Mates, would take all of the last night, and the ship would have to wait to sail until it was completed.

The Chief Officer, meanwhile, would be responsible for ensuring the stability of the loaded ship, that she was not below her allowed waterline, had a suitable trim fore and aft without listing to port or starboard, and would, with some ballasting, be able to remain upright throughout the voyage, despite the anticipated discharge and loading of cargo along the way. The proper distribution of cargo was a complicated but crucial mathematical task in those days as modern sophisticated computer systems for making all the necessary loading calculations had yet to be introduced.

Outward bound our ship would carry a certain amount of bulk cargo such as bagged cement, heavy machinery, cars, tools, clothing, toy goods, foodstuffs and spirits. This was, of course, in the days before cargo became containerised, but valuable goods, beer and spirits were loaded into special lockers wherever possible because stevedores at all ports regarded them as fair game. It was common practice for gangs of stevedores to drop a case deliberately in order to break it open and pilfer the contents. One of the ship's officers would always be on duty to keep an eye on the cargo but it was often considered expedient to let them plunder an already broken case of, say, whisky in order to save the rest of the batch.

When discharging cargo with the ship's own derricks the 'union purchase', a combination of two wires shackled together from each of two winches, was commonly used. Two winchmen worked the wires slung through blocks, heaving in or paying out at their respective derrick heads, to control the swinging pallet or cradle. Cars were normally stowed in the tweendecks and would be lifted out by cradle, one derrick being positioned to plumb the hatch, the other overside. But it was not unknown for a car cradle to swing against the steel hatch coaming while being lifted in or out, with disastrous results.

One item of cargo that caused particular interest was a Silver Ghost Rolls-Royce loaded in Liverpool and destined for Alfred Hitchcock in Los Angeles. This Rolls-Royce had to be handled with extreme care as, immaculate and gleaming in the Californian sun, it was lifted from the hold between two derricks and swung over the hatch coaming unscratched in a cradle.

Homeward bound we made most use of the refrigerated chambers which were arranged on three deck levels, typically to carry fresh fruit including boxed apples from British Columbia and citrus fruit loaded in Oakland and San Francisco. Additionally bananas and other fruit would be loaded in Kingston, Jamaica. On the weather deck and sometimes in the shelter deck we would carry lumber from Vancouver, New Westminster and Seattle. Again we found wood an awkward cargo to carry on deck because it absorbed moisture, so raising the ship's centre of gravity and could cause the ship to list a few degrees to port or starboard.

A 1912 Silver Ghost Rolls-Royce for Alfred Hitchcock being unloaded from *Loch Loyal* in Los Angeles. *(Author's photo 1959)*

I stayed with the *Loch Loyal* until November 1959, when I was promoted to Second Officer to sail again in the old *Brittany*. We set off for the West Indies and then through Panama to the west coast of Central America, calling at small picturesque harbours among the wooded hills in Nicaragua, El Salvador and Guatemala, to pick up bales of cotton and hemp. Sometimes the ship would lie at anchor and load from lighters, sometimes from the shore.

It was always interesting to visit these places off the beaten track where oceangoing ships were rarely seen, and most of the local population would find some excuse to come aboard. In one small port, I forget which, where there was an evident shortage of young men, mothers brought their attractive Latin-American teenage daughters on board in the hope of finding suitable spouses for them among the crew. But, alas, our stays were all too short, sometimes just a few hours, as we worked our way down the coast, loading the local produce in the steaming tropical heat.

In those cargo vessels, the Second Officer kept the 12–4 'graveyard' night watch and afternoon watch. Principally he was responsible to the Master for the navigation of the ship, laying of all courses on each voyage, consulting the Admiralty Tide Tables wherever necessary for sea currents and safe depths of water, and for correcting the charts from Admiralty Notices to Mariners. This latter task was an arduous ongoing duty involving making corrections, typically to positions of navigation marks, changes to lights or additions of wrecks; all done by hand in purple indelible ink. As Notices were issued every week, they were brought on board in suitable ports by the ship's agent. Although this is a dull chore, accuracy is all important, and there have been many cases of shipwreck over the years due to failure or inaccuracy in correcting charts. So that was something for the Second Mate to worry about, although we did have a system for sending our relevant chart portfolios ashore to hydrographic agents at the end of each voyage so that they could be brought fully up to date.

Entering and leaving port the Second Officer was stationed aft on the poop deck where he directed the crew and shore gangs in mooring and casting off lines. The danger here was the ultimate horror of getting mooring lines entangled in the propeller. Before departure from a berth it was normal practice to 'single up' from three to just one stern line and a spring line leading forward. Similarly the Chief Officer singled up forward. On the telephoned order from the bridge to 'let go' the two stern lines would be cast off by the shore gang and they had to be hauled in on the barrels of the ship's winches as quickly as possible so that the ship's engines could be used to steer the vessel clear of the quayside.

No cargo ship carrying up to twelve passengers was obliged to carry a doctor. In Royal Mail it was the practice for the Second Officer to act as ship's doctor, though in other shipping lines it might be the Chief Officer's or Chief Steward's responsibility. There was an infirmary, complete with a medicine chest, including various surgical tools, needle and thread. Also a *Shipmaster's Medical Guide* liberally illustrated with lurid pictures of nasty tropical diseases. Armed with these one had to do the best one could. In the time that I served as Second Officer in the *Brittany* and *Eden* I was relieved to have no major emergencies on my hands. By now I was regretting the very superficial way I had skimmed through the preparation for my First Aid Certificate while taking Second Mate's exams, and I lived in fear of being faced with a major accident. In fact, we were seldom at sea for more ten days at a time and it was normal to refer patients with any lasting problems to the doctor in each port. Meanwhile one used penicillin injections for sexually transmitted diseases and other infections, while aspirin, kaolin stomach mixture, and cough mixture, iodine and plasters took care of most other daily problems. One had to watch the supply of Gee's Linctus cough mixture, though, as sailors could become rather addicted to it.

It was normal to hold a surgery half-hour once a day at sea and, when necessary, in port. The West Indian stevedores liked to come with their cuts and bruises; I found that a liberal application of iodine made them feel that they had been taken seriously.

I did once have an engineer report sick with a severe infection in one ear which worried me as we were not due in port for several days; however, following a recommendation in the *Medical Guide*, I dripped surgical spirit on cotton wool into his ear; apparently he was in agony all night but the infection did disappear. I did not look forward to having to stitch wounds; however, I never had to do worse than take out stitches which had been put in by a shore doctor. For treating minor wounds or removing splinters a simple aerosol anaesthetic was effective in numbing the local area and, wisely, no crew member ever asked me to extract a tooth, although we had the basic equipment in the medicine chest.

While on leave from my voyages in the *Brittany* in July 1960 I was unexpectedly telegrammed by the company asking me to help bring the cargo ship *Araby* round from Liverpool to Swansea because the National Union of Seamen had called a strike leaving ships stranded in various ports. So, along with several other company officers who had also been on leave, I signed on the *Araby* for three days, ostensibly as a 'Deck Officer', but in fact to make up deck crew in order to take the ship out of Liverpool docks on the night tide. I was, along with other members of our scratch crew, handling the mooring lines and working the winch aft as our ship crept out through the locks to the cry of 'scabs' from those dockworkers who had spotted us. We used the sailors' accommodation and had a very informal and rather jolly time under the eye of the regular ship's officers, while taking the wheel and working on deck as we had learnt to during our various apprenticeships. This *Araby*, built in 1947 at Lithgows, Port Glasgow, was a sistership to the *Brittany* which I had just left. We berthed in Swansea Docks without incident on the 17th July and then, having been rewarded with double pay for three days, I enjoyed three weeks' summer leave before my next appointment to a passenger-carrying cargo ship on the West Indies run.

Particularly popular among crews and passengers were Royal Mail's E-boats, four of which were built by Harland & Wolff between 1952 and 1956. I was now fortunate to make a West Indian voyage as Second Officer on the latest of these, *Eden*, in August 1960. Making speeds of about 14 knots these 7,790-grt four-hatch cargo ships would make fairly leisurely three-month round voyages to Bermuda, Jamaica and other islands such as Dominica, carrying general cargo and returning with fruit and sugar. Passenger accommodation was luxurious and the food excellent.

The ports of call were lively and colourful to visit as only the West Indies can be. Kingston, Jamaica was, like Buenos Aires on the South American service, a sort of home from home. We were always greeted noisily and cheerfully by the native population. Among them were characters such as the robust Ella, who was typically swathed in flowing headscarf, bursting

RMS *Eden*, one of Royal Mail's popular E-boats serving the West Indies.

blouse and loose skirts which displayed every colour of the rainbow. She would be standing on the quay to greet every Royal Mail ship as it came alongside with her baskets of fresh produce piled with luscious ripe pineapples, bananas and avocados to bargain with or sell. And when the stevedores swarmed on board the noise levels would rise with laughter and arguments in a patois that was hardly recognisable as English. Yet when working down the holds storing cargo, particularly during the night shifts, there would at times for just a few minutes be a sudden down-tools hush followed by the melodious sound of negro spirituals echoing round the lower decks.

Rather regretfully I paid off from *Eden* in November that year, as she was one of the finest ships I sailed in, but it was time for Christmas leave and to go up for my Master's Certificate, which I would do while remaining under contract to Royal Mail. This involved another term's study at Sir John Cass College, which provided a welcome break in London, where I again stayed at the Merchant Navy Hotel in Lancaster Gate.

While at college I took the opportunity to take my driving test in London's East End and it was there that I bought my first car, a 1937 Morris Ten, for just £25. Despite its age the car was really quite smart with its leather seats and chromium-plated radiator and headlamps. It could even do 70 mph at a pinch but the wiring in the steering column had an embarrassing habit of short-circuiting when I made a sharp turn so that the horn would blow loud and long until I switched off the engine. I was very attached to this car but eventually had to abandon it to the nearest garage when, on driving cross-country on the day before the end of a period of leave, all the oil drained out and the big end went. Cars acquired by me on following leaves were also to suffer ignominious fates. A fine-looking Triumph Mayflower, left in a barn on a neighbour's farm when I was recalled from leave one time, never wanted to go again on my return. The field mice had had too good a time.

In later years I acquired a second-hand Austin Healey 'frog-eye' Sprite, a handsome blackberry-coloured open-top which I thoroughly enjoyed driving. It lasted for several years and was at its best in the long hot summer of 1976 but let snow in above the windshield in winter weather. For fun I even took frog-eye along on the London to Brighton veteran car run. We had a tremendous downpour that day; I've often had to bail out boats but that was the only time I and my luckless lady passenger had to bail out a car. Frog-eye also eventually suffered an inglorious fate, having been stored for too long in a barn, and I was obliged to sell her for her number plate 'OCL 800' to one of the management of the Overseas Container Line who duly sent down an OCL lorry to pick her up.

A Master's ticket was the final Board of Trade qualification needed to command a ship; one had to have done seven years actual sea time. Studies for Masters included navigation, seamanship, ship stability and cargo handling, taking these subjects a step further than for the Mates' tickets, as well as shipmaster's business. One was also retested on eyesight and signalling. It was a proud achievement to become a Master Mariner, although an actual appointment as ship's Master, or Captain, was still many years away if one was serving in most of the established shipping fleets sailing under the Red Ensign, if not under flags of convenience.

8

The South American Liners Aragon and Amazon

RMS *Aragon* built 1960. One of three identical sisterships for the South American service.

With my brand new Master's ticket I signed on the latest Royal Mail liner, *Aragon*, in the comparatively lowly rank of Junior Third Officer in April 1961. This 'Junior Third' rank reflected the fact that watches were doubled up on these larger passenger–cargo ships, more deck officers were needed and all were required to hold Master's certificates. A far cry indeed from tramp ships under flags of convenience where just one Master's Certificate, often from a doubtful source, was considered sufficient qualification to be held aboard a foreign-going ship.

The A-boats came with a very much more demanding range of duties than a simple cargo ship. For a start there was responsibility for the safe passage of several hundred passengers, often including VIPs, and several nationalities of crew, again in the hundreds, together with the accompanying safety and life-saving equipment and the procedures that this entailed. Then there was a full range of cargoes including heavy lifts, valuable goods, frozen, chilled or perishable, to be carried between port and port, as well as responsibility for transporting diplomatic mails and bullion, all in the one multi-purpose liner. The Captain himself was usually very taken up with social duties and officialdom in foreign ports while the Chief Officer was responsible for the overall smooth running and ship discipline as well as the very complicated distribution of cargo and stability of the ship. The Senior Second Officer (4–8 watch) would therefore be the navigator and senior watchkeeping officer at sea while the Junior Second (12–4) and Senior Third (8–12) were the other two watchkeepers, with the Junior Third assisting on the busy daybreak watch.

The *Amazon, Aragon* and *Arlanza*, could each carry up to 107 first-class, 82 cabin-class and 275 third-class passengers, each class with its own public rooms, catering facilities, and open deck areas including built-in open-air tiled swimming pools. With five cargo hatches and four cargo decks a large proportion of space was given over to chambers for carrying chilled and frozen meat homeward from the River Plate. There were also strong rooms for carrying bullion, and separate rooms for mailbags and passenger baggage.

The Amazon-class ships soon became very popular with their officers and crews for good reason. The voyages were particularly interesting for the great variety in the types passengers and cargoes they carried, also the exotic nature of the ports of call such as Rio de Janeiro, Santos, Montevideo and Buenos Aires. We had excellent accommodation, enjoyed mainly benign weather, particularly during the seven-day relaxed Atlantic crossing between Las Palmas and Rio, and the voyages were of a very civilised length overall, allowing us all to get home on leave for about a week once in every two months. Conditions on board were undoubtedly the best I had known in all my time at sea.

We followed a similar itinerary to the previous *Highland* boats, leaving with general cargo from the Royal Docks, though we now called at Tilbury overnight to pick up our passengers, also tying up at a pier in Cherbourg to load mailbags before carrying on to Vigo and Lisbon where, after three to four days, we would disembark a few cabin-class passengers going on holiday, their cars having been stowed on deck. In those ports we would also take on Spanish and Portuguese emigrants for Argentina and Brazil respectively and other passengers, together with the catering staff to look after them. Two days later we docked at Las Palmas to load and discharge mail and for bunkering. This gave the passengers a few hours ashore before we sailed that evening on our Atlantic crossing, our next landfall to be the Brazilian coast a week later.

Our arrival to drop anchor in the spectacular bay of Rio de Janeiro was always timed for 0600 hours and would precede a hectic day discharging general cargo, mail, baggage and passengers before taking on new passengers for the two-day run down to Montevideo and then on up the River Plate to Buenos Aires. There we discharged all remaining passengers, cargo and mail, cleaned the holds, cooled down refrigerated chambers and moved on to berths alongside the *frigorificos* to load chilled and frozen beef carcasses before going back to South Dock in Buenos Aires to take on our passengers for the homeward run. This whole process normally took eight days; then we retraced our course homeward, via Montevideo, Santos, Rio, Las Palmas, Lisbon, Vigo and the Ocean Terminal in Southampton where we landed our passengers, before making our way up the Thames to the Royal Docks to discharge our chilled and frozen meat.

This was the first ship in which I had experienced the use of stabilisers to dampen the ship's rolling motion; these were Denny-Brown retractable gyro-controlled fins on either side of the hull which would reduce rolling to as little as a degree or two at most. They could be extended hydraulically by simply turning a key on the navigating bridge. This was generally done once the pilot had disembarked and the ship was 'full away' in deep water; the fins would not have been effective at slow speeds or in shallow water. They would be kept extended during the voyage, except in the calmest of weather when they might be retracted because their frictional resistance to water flow would reduce the ship's speed by almost one half-knot. As the stabilisers would have to be retracted when reducing speed to approach port, there were occasions when, encountering a heavy swell on crossing a bar or turning at the harbour entrance, the ship would roll unexpectedly and take passengers and crew completely by surprise with the risk of damage to limb and crockery. It was normal therefore for the officer of the watch to warn passengers over the Tannoy when there was danger of this happening.

I recall just one accident when in mid-ocean, sadly, a whale, drifting idly down the ship's side, was hit by the port fin. This shook the whole 20,000-ton ship and one can only imagine what it did to the whale left behind in our swirling bloodied wake.

Having a large catering crew and many opportunities to load victuals in European and South American ports made for an excellent menu; our itinerary allowed us to enjoy a lot of fresh fruit and vegetables, also the best Argentine beef. We junior officers received silver service in the cabin-class dining room. Then there was the luxury of the swimming pools, which we were free to enjoy when off duty in company with cabin-class passengers, as well as the entertainments on board including the bars and dancing. But the very best entertainment, enthusiastically encouraged by the ship's staff, was provided by the many young and lively passengers themselves, in many cases enjoying the trip of a lifetime.

There were traditional strong links between the UK and South America. Many of the large estancias in Argentina were owned by families of British stock, who, together with many others who had helped to build the infra-structure of Argentina, went to make up the bilingual Anglo-Argentine commu-nity: these tended to travel back and forth between the two continents by ship. There were school leavers coming from Argentina, Chile and Brazil to spend the summer in England and Europe, then returning three months later. There were diplomats and their families; there were the families of men going out to new jobs in South America, notably with oil companies, banks or engi-neering consultancies; there were single teenagers going out to visit relatives in South America. Then there were the migrants from Portugal, going to start new lives in Brazil, and from Spain on their way to Uruguay or Argentina. Homeward bound we tended to carry a smaller number of Argentines and Brazilians returning to visit their roots. Arriving and departing from each port was always a moment of excitement frequently accompanied by the drama of tearful welcomes and goodbyes among the passengers and their families and friends.

On my very first voyage aboard the *Aragon* we had on board eighteen Chilean girls, school leavers with their music mistress, coming to England to enjoy the summer months. This was the adventure of their lives. Several of them had English or Scottish ancestry, typically with names such as Cameron or Mackenzie, although the families were well mixed with Latin American blood. There was not one of these girls who was not a beauty. They all sang and some played the guitar, so night after night, we were treated to breathtaking entertainment on deck under the stars as the ship passed through the tropics, gliding on its way across the Atlantic towards Europe. I don't think any of us, and certainly not our passengers, wanted to see an end to that all-too-short Atlantic crossing between the southern and northern hemispheres. The ship would roll very gently, causing the stars to swing overhead as we sat out in the balmy air, listening to this sponta-neous music and song. Imagine in the background, the hum of the engines and swish of water breaking away from the ship's sides with phosphores-cent ripples as the 20,000-ton ship pushed her way through the smooth waters of the doldrums at 17 knots.

After two voyages in *Aragon* I took some leave and then did a spell of relief duty around the UK coast as Second Mate of a Royal Mail cargo ship, *Tuscany*, working between such ports as London, Liverpool and Newport. It was usual between ship postings to do relieving duties, thus enabling other

Enjoying the company of Chilean passengers, *Aragon* 1961.

officers to take leave from their ships while in home waters. It also had the advantage of keeping officers circulating among different types and classes of ship, thus getting to know the other company officers and petty officers, and becoming familiar with many different types of cargo. Typically in *Tuscany* we would have been discharging sugar at Tate & Lyle's wharf in the London Docks, coasting round to Liverpool to load general cargo and cars, then down to Newport to load steelwork. Coasting was no holiday as it involved turning out at all hours of day or night to dock and undock with tugs in the various ports and having to become familiar with the layout and cargo arrangements of unfamiliar ships.

Then to my delight I was re-appointed to another A-boat, the *Amazon*, as Senior Third Officer. This meant that I was the 8–12 watchkeeper and cargo officer; this is the most civilised watch to keep from the point of view of duty hours and sleep, although it did mean missing out on evening entertainment with the passengers at sea. There was plenty of this including films, dances and generally mingling with the passengers in the Bamboo Bar, the name given to the cosy cabin-class bar which junior officers were permitted to use, and where many of the first-class passengers also congregated. One just hoped that many an impromptu party would still be in full swing when one came off duty at midnight, safe in the knowledge that one could catch

Amazon alongside in Cherbourg with *Queen Mary* astern. *(Author's photo 1963)*

up on lost sleep during the following afternoon siesta. The siesta, other-wise known as a 'deckhead survey', was a tradition among all off-duty watch-keepers, a couple of hours usually uninterrupted until fire, lifeboat or accident drill was held around 1600.

When I came off watch at night I myself would head straight away for a quick dip, floating on my back in the cabin-class pool and watching the mast overhead slowly gyrating against the canopy of stars.

Watchkeeping, although not arduous in the open sea, was never an easy discipline as it was essential to be on the ball all the time. For four hours on continuous duty the watchkeeping officer had to be the eyes and ears of the ship. Though on one's feet and confined to the bridge for this entire time, there would frequently be little to do, particularly at night when in the open ocean, beyond keeping an eye out for other ships, filling in the weather conditions in the ship's log and probably sending off a meteorological report to the Meteorological Office at Bracknell.

The officer of the watch was required to make weather reports every six hours in those days; this involved recording air pressure, visibility, tempera-ture, humidity, cloud, wind and sea conditions in a coded message which was then sent off in Morse to the Met Office by the ship's duty radio operator. From these reports, sent at the same six-hourly Greenwich Mean Time by selected ships scattered across the oceans, the Met Office would build up its Atlantic and other weather maps every day. In the days before satellite pictures did the job for us, Met reports would become particularly significant during the hurricane season in that part of the Atlantic popularly known as the Bermuda Triangle, for they could give clear indications of a hurricane building up and help to track its path.

The tracks typically taken by hurricanes were treated very seriously. They are not entirely predictable but have a tendency to make a distinct turn northwards after moving west, so the mariner has to navigate his ship to avoid being caught unawares. This could easily happen if the ship should be in what is known as the dangerous sector to the north of the eye of the hurricane.

A sharp reminder of the need to keep a keen lookout, even when in open seas and clear weather, struck me one day when on watch. Eye level from the wheelhouse of a large passenger ship like the *Amazon* is some 60 feet or 20 metres above sea level, with the horizon just about 8 miles away. Another ship approaching could of course even be seen 'hull down' on the horizon several miles beyond that; so, it would seem plenty of time to foresee any impending problem with oncoming traffic at sea.

It was one of those bright sunny mornings on the 8–12 watch with a brilliant-blue sea peppered with white-capped waves in a fresh wind, when I was enjoying the air on the bridge wing and keeping an eye out for the first signs of land. We were nearing our Brazilian landfall of Cape Frio, but still, according to the estimated position from that morning's star sights, at least 20 miles off the coast. This was to be our first landfall after crossing the Atlantic on the approach to Rio de Janeiro. For several days at sea we had seen nothing more than the occasional distant ship or smoke on the horizon and, as I scanned the horizon, I was more concerned about fixing our position from the expected sighting of land for the first time in over a week. With a sudden shock I saw on either side of the ship, already too close ahead to take any evasive action, a scattering of four of five small open fishing boats with just two men in each. I could hardly believe my eyes. They were too low to have shown against the horizon visually or on the radar and were partially obscured by the white-capped waves all around. One might well wonder what these small boats were doing so far from land; the answer was that they had been launched from a mother ship which was standing off a few miles away. These fearless fishermen were taking advantage of a prime fish catchment area to fish during the day off Cape Frio, so named because it is where the cold current runs up from the far south to that knuckle of the Brazilian coast where it meets the warmer waters of the tropical Atlantic, thus providing fruitful fishing. With relief I saw this small fleet of boats pass safely down on either side of our ship, the fishermen looking up at us apparently unconcerned, again to be lost bobbing away among the waves in our wake.

After fixing our position from bearings of Cape Frio and the coastline, we would adjust course and speed as necessary, taking the currents into account, to make our expected time of arrival (ETA) in the bay at Rio de Janeiro around 0600 hours the following morning. During the preceding night there would, if the weather was clear and not foggy, be a spectacular distant sighting of the Corcovada statue of *Christ the Redeemer*, arms outstretched, floodlit and standing in the hills high above Rio. Gleaming silvery in the starlight, this provided a dramatic and easily recognised navigational lead to our destination.

Arriving as dawn broke in the bay of Rio de Janeiro through a narrow waterway between two small islands was always spectacular. To the left was the high peak of the nearby Sugarloaf, and all round a ring of heavily wooded mountains, dominated by the vast stone statue of Christ blessing the city. Along the curves of the famous Copacabana and Ipanema beaches was a fringe of skyscrapers, suggesting wealth and luxury. These contrasted with the *favelas*, or settlements of shacks, inhabited by the very poor, which stretched up into the forested hills behind. With the sunrise the whole city came alive, and this was indeed the most vibrant city I ever saw. With all flags flying, we were met by the pilot boat, quarantine, immigration and customs, the agent's boat bringing the ship's mail, and a host of workboats, and we let out our anchor chain with a roar to await our berth alongside close to the city centre. Once on the quay we would be faced with one long busy day, discharging passengers, cars, general cargo, bullion such as silver bars and registered mailbags; by the afternoon, we would have to be ready to take on new passengers for the run down to the River Plate. Meanwhile the transit passengers would be free to visit the town with its colourful shops, particularly jewellers' selling gemstones, amber or local semi-precious stones such as amethyst, or to go to the fabulous sandy beaches where the populace sunned themselves, the girls in miniscule bikinis, and where youths played endless games of football, or to go on excursions up the Sugarloaf or to the Corcovada by cable car to experience the stunning views.

On one occasion, due to a port strike, our Master, Captain Grant, in order to keep to our schedule, made the decision to take the *Amazon* out of Rio without tugs or help from shore labour on the quay. It was a tricky manoeuvre in a large ship, involving casting off mooring lines, with which Brazilian naval volunteers assisted, and moving away from the quay without damaging the hull plating and then turning the bow into the buoyed channel. In those days ships did not have side thrusters to help them when manoeuvring. This manoeuvre, however, went smoothly enough and was well recorded in the local press.

Leaving Rio at sunset we would sail overnight south-west down the coast to Santos, again arriving early morning, this time up a steamy winding wooded river, where the discharging and loading procedures would be repeated.

Santos was very much a commercial working port and we, the crew, rarely got further than the dock area ourselves. Passengers could go to the nearby Guaraja beach, take excursions to a snake farm or go further inland to Brazil's fast-expanding business capital of São Paulo. Brasilia, the new official capital of Brazil, some 500 miles to the north, had not yet come into its own. When we crew had time to go ashore, should there be an overnight stay, it was to dockside bars and restaurants of an evening. There was one simple white-tiled restaurant I will never forget for the incongruous but highly talented string trio of Romanian immigrants who played the most soul-rending music. The food – we usually indulged in steaks with an egg and red wine or beer – was excellent and very cheap in these unsophisticated restaurants, but there could be trouble also. I went ashore with a group of deck officers and engineers one evening for such a meal. We had paid our bill with a fistful of cruzeiros and were finishing off our last drinks when the woman behind the counter accused us of not having paid and threatened to send for the police; we refused to pay again on principle and a policeman did suddenly appear. This was obviously a put-up job to extract more money from us and while we continued to refuse, a kindly American at the next table who was familiar with the area paid up for us, although much against our wishes. We told him not to, but he replied that we did not know what the inside of a Brazilian jail was like and we would have been certain to have spent one night there at the very least.

From Santos it was a two-day run on down to Montevideo at the mouth of the River Plate for a short stop before going up that muddy river to our terminal destination of Buenos Aires.

Among the most interesting passengers we carried were fifty islanders returning to their native Tristan da Cunha, which, with the aid of the Royal Navy, they had hastily evacuated in the wake of volcanic eruptions on the island many months earlier. Keen to be going home after living in camps in the English Home Counties, they boarded *Amazon* at Tilbury in March 1963, to trans-ship in Montevideo. These were quiet, dignified, dusky-skinned and very simple people who spent most of their time playing cards or knitting in *Amazon's* third-class lounge.

Homeward bound, one voyage in August 1963 we called at Vigo to discharge passengers and some frozen meat, but struck a knuckle on the quay as we berthed. A double-bottom ballast tank pipe was ruptured, causing the ship to take on an apparently alarming list against the wharf. The local radio was quick to latch on to this embarrassing incident and people flocked down to watch *Amazon* 'sinking in the harbour'. In fact, the incident was not serious, and after transferring some ballast we were soon on our way.

A change of routine came with my appointment as Junior Second Officer in October 1963, which involved taking over the 12–4 or 'graveyard' watch while most of the ship slept, and doing night duty in port. This was never so popular because of the disruption of sleeping patterns, but after four further voyages I was promoted to Senior Second Officer in September 1964 for my thirteenth voyage in *Amazon*. I was now the senior watchkeeper and navigator on board, and was also responsible for directing the quartermaster's duties, which involved the upkeep of the bridge, flags, signalling and lifesaving equipment. Another specific duty was responsibility for safe carriage in the strong rooms of bullion and mail and discharging them in their respective ports. This involved tallying each mailbag, of which several hundred were still carried by sea in those days. Bullion usually constituted bars of silver, for the protection of which I was issued in the early days with a revolver; this however, I never had to produce in anger. Mail, for which I had to obtain receipts, included red bags of registered mail and piles of hessian bags of ordinary sea mail. Any discrepancy in the tallies would involve letters from head office as, after all, mail had originally been the *raison d'être* of Royal Mail Lines.

General cargo and mail for the Falkland Islands were normally discharged in Montevideo for trans-shipping, as Argentina was always very sensitive about the sovereignty of these islands. There was one occasion when we had on board 260 bags of mail for the Falklands but, owing to a stevedoring strike in Montevideo, we were unable to discharge the mail there during our one-day stopover, and the agent told me to carry it on to Buenos Aires where it was unloaded along with all the Argentine mail. Unfortunately the mail for the Falklands was never delivered; we heard later from our agents that all the mail for the Falklands had been sifted and those not addressed to the 'Islas Malvinas', which was probably the lot, were burnt. There was a very nasty letter from Head Office.

Opportunities for the crew to exercise in the actual use of lifeboats were rare, but we were encouraged to launch and row them when there was time in the various docks we visited. There was always one motor lifeboat on board a ship, this being the accident-and-recovery boat; otherwise they were manoeuvred under oars, though the latest A-boats had manually levered propeller propulsion which had obvious advantages over oars in manoeuvring to and from the ship's side. Lifeboats were also provided with a single mast and heavy canvas lugsail, which could be of use in the open sea if not trying to sail close to the wind. Although in practice I never had the experience of sailing a lifeboat, we had learnt the theory of rigging and sailing lifeboats for our exams and, of course lifeboat sails had been instrumental in saving countless lives among seamen whose ships had been torpedoed in mid-ocean during the war years. Running before the prevailing winds, such as the north-east or south-east trades, a boat could make a steady 3–4 knots, covering up to 100 miles a day.

On one occasion, while in mid-Atlantic on a fine sunny day, we were carrying out a routine accident boat drill. While keeping the 4–8 afternoon watch I set off the accident boat drill alarm at the appointed time, after warning the passengers over the Tannoy that this was merely a crew drill. Following normal routine the accident boat's crew mustered at the motor lifeboat station on the starboard side below the bridge wearing their life jackets. On order from the Captain, who had joined me on the bridge, the motor boat was lowered to deck level. Under the standard system of gravity davits a lifeboat will automatically slide down the bow and stern trackways of the davits once the retaining pins have been removed and the winch brake lever lifted.

The sailors detailed to man the accident boat duly embarked at deck level, wearing life jackets. Then, all being in order, they disembarked while two able seamen remained in the boat as the bosun used the electric winch to raise the boat again by winding in the wire falls fore and aft. But on this occasion the wire rove through the aft fall blocks suddenly broke and with an almighty crash the lifeboat swung vertically down, hanging from the bow hook alone on the forward falls. The two sailors were instantly thrown out and fell thirty feet into the sea. The ship meanwhile was still steaming ahead at 18 knots. So I had to ring stop engines immediately while the Captain gave the order 'hard a starboard' and we turned to retrieve them. They were both shaken but unharmed when, a few minutes later, they were picked up in a real-life accident drill, now using the port-side boat, the only thing lost being one lifebuoy bobbing away in the ship's wake. The passengers were most impressed by this realistic boat drill.

Stowaways, usually single men without any papers, could be a serious nuisance because once on board it was very hard to get rid of them. Immigration authorities would not let them land in foreign ports and the ship's Master would be held responsible for seeing that they did not get ashore. On one Stanhope ship we had carried, for many months, a harmless young man we'd picked up in a small eastern oil port. He was quiet enough and worked with the crew. Eventually the Captain allowed him to 'escape' shortly before leaving a Brazilian port.

On the passenger ships of the Royal Mail South American service it was normal for the Chief Officer to organise a stowaway search about half an hour before leaving port. But stowaway searches were far from foolproof, considering that dozens of passengers disembarked in Brazilian ports such as Rio or Santos to be replaced by a hundred or more travelling third class down to Argentina. The face of a stowaway boarding while the last of the stevedores were handling baggage and cargo could be lost among the faces of new passengers. Provided a stowaway did not do the obvious, like attempting to hide in a lifeboat, he might not be detected for a day or more.

One fine day at sea I was called upon to take the motor lifeboat away to transfer a stowaway from the *Amazon* to our homeward-bound sistership, *Arlanza*, as the two ships were due to pass one another between Santos in Brazil and Montevideo in Uruguay. The most convenient thing to do with a stowaway would be to send him back whence he came, and so it was that our then Captain, R.D. Jones, decided to transfer this luckless young man, found wandering the decks late on the night we left Santos southbound, to our sistership, which was due to dock there the following day.

The morning dawned fine with a relatively smooth sea but also with a long low Atlantic swell. I had as usual sent the quartermaster to call the Captain and inform him of the weather conditions at 0600 hours. He came to the bridge and immediately instructed the duty radio officer to contact the *Arlanza* for her position. Sure enough we were due to pass one another around breakfast time. Ours was the senior Captain, so never mind the sea swell and nuisance to *Arlanza*, we would have a jolly good boat drill and give the passengers some interest by stopping and lowering a boat with the stowaway aboard to transfer him to the other ship. We reduced speed as RMS *Arlanza* was seen steaming over the horizon on our port bow in the hazy morning sunshine. I, being now off the bridge watch and therefore available, was detailed to take the boat away at 0900 hours.

When the poor man, who spoke no English, was given a life jacket and made to board the lifeboat out in the open sea he must have wondered what on earth his fate would be and was visibly trembling. I, meanwhile, was looking with some concern at the sea swell rising and falling lazily over a range of some 10 feet against the ship's side. However, the Captain turned the ship to give a lee; I boarded with my crew, the boat was lowered and we set off under engine power for the rapidly approaching liner. I was a little alarmed when it appeared that she had slowed but had no intention of stopping. A ladder was thrown over as we in the boat sidled up to the liner's port side under full throttle to keep pace with her; then two sailors stood by to heave the reluctant stowaway onto the rungs of the rope ladder the moment our boat brushed alongside her hull plating.

Transferring a stowaway by lifeboat off the Brazilian coast. *(Photo from Amazon)*

It was with relief that I put the helm hard over to turn away and head back to our ship. But securing a boat again by the hooks on the heavy steel blocks of the falls fore and aft can be dangerous, as this is done manually while the lifeboat rides up and down on the sea swell. A clout on the head from one of these blocks can cause serious injury and the stability of the boat is threatened if both falls are not engaged simultaneously. We succeeded tolerably well at the second attempt and after our *Amazon* was underway again Captain Bolland of *Arlanza* was good enough to send a telegram congratulating me on my handling the boat alongside. Little did he know I had never handled a lifeboat in open water in my life before. And our Chief Officer was not so pleased that I had not recovered the stowaway's life jacket after he boarded the other ship, though how I was supposed to do this was a mystery to me. Our inventory of lifesaving equipment would now be one life jacket short, which just shows that you can't please everybody all the time.

Leaving the terminal port on a passenger ship was always accompanied by a lot of waving, blaring of taped music over the loudspeaker, flag flying and throwing of streamers between shore and ship, very often with not a few tears as well, as relatives and friends were about to become separated indefinitely. One occasion stands out in my memory. We were leaving the dockside in Buenos Aires, with tugs attached to pull us off and our mooring lines singled up forward and aft. Then bow and stern lines were cast off and we nudged about 15 feet away from the quay but moved only sluggishly in the bubbling brown water till the ship stuck fast in soft mud. The music continued to play and the passengers and their friends and relatives to wave at one another, as our propellers churned away. After a good ten minutes of this, when it became obvious that we were getting no further from the quayside, the waving died down, the taped music was switched off and a silence descended on all the assembled company as it dawned on everyone that we were sitting firmly on the mud. Touching bottom is actually not an uncommon experience in the River Plate; the mud is light and shifts easily and it is usually only necessary to wait patiently for a foot or so rise in tide. Ships' hulls designed to navigate in the River Plate are of a rounded bottom section, which makes re-floating easy. In the event we slid quietly away from the berth in the gathering dusk about an hour after all those who had come to see us off had melted away.

But it was not always so simple and there were serious dangers in navigating through mud in narrow parts of the shallow, buoyed channel of the River Plate, as was most tragically demonstrated several years later. Two British cargo ships under the Red Ensign belonging to the respected family firm Houlder Line, namely the 10,000-dwt *Royston Grange* and her sister, *Hardwicke Grange*, had, like our A-boats, been specifically designed and built for the UK–River Plate refrigerated trade in 1959–60 and could carry up to twelve passengers. We were very familiar with these attractive 498ft ships with which we frequently met up or passed by during our voyages.

It was years later, after the Royal Mail ships had ceased running to the River Plate, that on 11th May 1972, owing to a build-up of mud in the channel, the *Royston Grange* was in collision with a Hong Kong tanker, *Tien Chee*, in the River Plate's Indio channel 40 miles south-west of Montevideo and nine miles from the Argentine coast. It is believed that the *Tien Chee* was actually ploughing through mud at the time while the lighter draught, *Royston Grange*, was skimming over it with her bilge keels just making contact. According to the formal investigation which followed, when the bows of the two ships were abreast of one another in a narrow shallow section of the channel, water pressure and suction due to lack of water depth caused the *Royston Grange* to veer to port and strike the *Tien Chee* just forward of amidships. Locked together with their port sides open, the two ships were engulfed in fire as oil from the tanker's ruptured cargo spaces ignited. The Houlder ship was burnt out, probably due to release of refrigerant gasses, and all seventy-four crew and ten passengers perished as well as the Argentine river pilot who was conning the ship. Meanwhile twenty-seven of the forty Chinese tanker crew escaped their ship by lifeboat.

From March 1962 until July 1965 I made seventeen round voyages with *Amazon*, and I would not have chosen to be in any other ship. During this time I had built up a large number of friends in Buenos Aires in particular. One never got leave to stay away from the ship as watches always had to be kept on board, but we could arrange the odd day off to meet people at the Yacht Club, Hurlingham Club or the Jockey Club, or even go to the local Harrods, all establishments of Anglo-Argentine heritage; or one might travel by suburban train to see friends in residential suburbs such as Olivos. Initially these trains comprised fine old wood-and-brass fitted carriages built in Britain some fifty years earlier. But in the early 1960s new rolling stock was introduced from Japan; unfortunately the height of the carriage doors in relation to the platform had not been considered in advance and wooden steps had incongruously to be placed manually on the platforms throughout the suburban network to bridge a gap in height of 2–3 feet.

If one travelled by the local buses, known as *collectivos*, the docks were a bumpy drive away from the main railway station of Buenos Aires which was the hub of the city's transport system. But the roads up to town, strewn with holes, were appalling and the *collectivos*, old and apparently without springs, did little to make for a smooth drive, nor did the drivers, who tried to imitate the great Argentine racing driver Fangio who, we were proudly told, had once been a *collectivo* driver himself. The station, Retiro, with its magnificent marble-halled bar–restaurant was itself a popular social meeting place to enjoy an aperitif. We would often also choose to eat out well on local beefsteaks at restaurants in La Boca, a slum dock area, which has since become far more fashionable.

Our social life with the residents of Buenos Aires was unfortunately distinctly hit-and-miss, and many a romance foundered, as one could never guarantee the ship's schedule or of being able to take time off. To add to our problems the local telephone system was appalling so that one would frequently be cut off while attempting to make contact with friends from the dockside phones.

We would normally load meat at three or four *frigorificos* in Buenos Aires, La Plata and finally Montevideo, including Hessian-wrapped bags of frozen beef and offal for the freezer chambers, muslin-wrapped sides of chilled beef which were slung from meat hooks in the cool rooms, and frozen lamb. These *frigorificos* provided a complete production line from the cattle slaughterhouse to the end product of chilled or frozen carcasses loaded aboard the ship berthed alongside.

I was once invited, along with the ship's doctor, to see over one of these meat factories in Buenos Aires. It was a grisly three-hour experience. The bullocks were delivered by lorry and, restless and frightened, herded into pens and guided towards a gate where, first, an electric rod was used to prod their necks, paralysing the muscles to keep them still. The animals were next stunned on the forehead with a special type of gun, chains slung round their rear legs, and lifted mechanically to hang head-down from a conveyor belt whereupon their throats were cut manually. Moving to the next station their bellies were slit open and their innards disgorged – at this stage there was a terrible stench and the ship's doctor was visibly sick. Next their carcasses were skinned and cut apart by skilled workers, and then washed prior to wrapping and stamping ready for shipping. Meanwhile the entrails, hooves and other bits all went their way for processing, eventually to provide bully beef, animal food and even glue. Nothing was wasted. On the very top floor of the building women in white coats stuffed freshly steamed 'bits' into cans by hand. The cans were sealed and sent down a chute which divided at a fork so that half the cans would come out as corned beef with the 'Armour' label and half with the 'Swift' label, the production of these two well-known brands having been recently merged.

The ship's doctor was never averse to a glass of whisky and that lunchtime I gratefully joined him to settle my stomach.

My Discharge Book shows that I was paid off from my last voyage in *Amazon* on 17th July 1965 in the Victoria Docks. I have in front of me now the yellowing pages of my Seaman's Discharge Book, that passport to go to sea, which records the date and place of every signing on and paying off ships from every seagoing voyage, together with a rubber-stamp report on character: for example 'Very good' (normal), 'Good' (which meant not so good) and 'DR' (decline to report, which meant very bad). This was signed and dated by the Captain at the end of each voyage.

The personality of the Captain himself has a huge bearing on the morale of the crew. As with all leaders he must strike a balance between discipline and concern for the welfare of the crew. *Amazon* had a reputation for being a happy ship, due in no small measure to Captain Grant RD RNR, by then Commodore of the Royal Mail fleet and affectionately known as Gentleman Grant, who – again I refer to my Discharge Book – was our Captain for thirteen consecutive voyages from my first signing on as *Amazon*'s Senior Third Officer in March 1962 until November 1964, when he retired. On his last homeward voyage in *Amazon*, he was given a tumultuous send off with flags and sirens from both Buenos Aires and Rio, an indication of just how much our ships were regarded as part of South American life.

It was a sad day for me when I finally had to pack up and leave *Amazon* after seventeen voyages in one of the best ships in the Royal Mail fleet. These had been my happiest days at sea but everyone has to move on sooner or later. I had been taken by surprise, however, and bitterly regretted that I had not had a chance to say goodbye to all the friends I had made over the years in South America.

I had leave due to me but, as my two-year contract was due to come up for renewal, and it was already becoming obvious that the writing was on the wall for Royal Mail's South American passenger and meat trade, I decided that this was the best time to make a break rather than face the anti-climax of a lifetime's seagoing in less interesting ships.

So I handed in my notice. This I did with very mixed feelings. On the one hand, I had been enjoying life; I was gaining seniority, had a clean record and the pay was not at all bad. On the other hand, like many others, I did not want permanently to be denied a home life. Importantly, too, the very ships, the way of life and the shipping company itself, were reaching the end of the road. The grand era of the passenger ship, mail ship and the general cargo ship was coming to an end to be replaced by air travel, bulk carriers, automated container ships and ever larger tankers. At the same time the British Merchant Navy, which had once dominated world transport and commerce, was already shrinking under the influence of flags of convenience, with the lower standards that entailed. I was soon proved right in supposing that Royal Mail Lines, in which I had originally chosen to make my career, would not survive independently for more than a few more years.

So in that summer of 1965, at the age of thirty-two, I returned on leave to my parents' new home in the hamlet of Lamarsh near Bures, a village set in the unspoilt Constable and Gainsborough country in the beautiful Stour Valley, bordering Essex and Suffolk. Having felt crowded out by house-building near Farnham in Surrey, they had bought an acre of land from a local farmer, and my sister, Rosanna, now a qualified architect, had designed the house to suit them. There, my retired father, now the Hon. Secretary of the Stour Valley Preservation Society, planned a garden to surround the house while my mother painted, threw pottery and sculpted in a small studio with the use of her own kiln.

I had to consider my future but, as my greatest interests still lay with the sea, I made enquiries initially of Southampton University in the hopes of studying for a degree in Oceanology. However, my seagoing Master's

9

To the French Riviera, then Back to Sea

The advertisement in the *Daily Telegraph* for a partner required to share in the ownership of a 10-metre motor yacht based in Cannes, to skipper it, and engage in the business of chartering, appealed enormously to my imagination and I answered the box number given. I received a very prompt telephone reply from Cannes. Being a Master Mariner, I was apparently just the person Mr Black, the owner, was looking for. I immediately flew out to Nice and went to meet Mr Black at a fashionable hotel. A well-fed and prosperous-looking man, he treated me to a good lunch on the terrace overlooking the sea and I was completely taken in by the ambiance of my surroundings. He wanted me to put up £2,200, which was quite a lot in those days but I had saved sufficient while at sea. Black regaled me with claims of how much could be earned by yacht chartering; it had, I knew, been a very lucrative business for those who had got in early.

I looked very carefully over the boat which was moored stern on in the old harbour at Cannes. She was a very genuine craft, an old 30-foot Belgian pilot boat now named the *Jane Mary* with an oak hull, teak decks and mahogany interior, two forward berths and a large central cabin containing two side berths as well as settees, all in good order. The wheelhouse being at the forward end of the main cabin had comfortable standing room and was resplendent with a huge solid-brass wheel and the portholes were of solid brass. The petrol engine was in good order and said to be capable of giving 12 knots. The *Jane Mary*'s logbook, known as the 'Green Card', was also in order.

So I slept alone on board that first night in August 1965, or rather lay awake listening to the gentle lap of water and creak of timbers, dreaming of what it would be like to own this boat on the Riviera. In the early hours I could hear small fish nibbling at the weed on the outer hull. In the morning the weather was glorious and, as the sun strengthened, I watched on as several boats got ready to sail out to the islands with picnic parties while, in the harbour, I spotted a few majestic sailing boats such as Errol Flynn's three-masted schooner, *Zorra*. So I fell for the proposition, and hurried, or rather *was* hurried, home to arrange my finances. This was my biggest mistake for, although, with a seaman's caution, I had carefully examined the boat and the seaworthiness of her hull, I had not had time to study the realistic prospects for chartering but merely taken Black's word.

Within forty-eight hours of returning to my parents' home in Suffolk I got a call from Mr Black checking that all was well and that I was going to be able to raise the money. He suggested, however, that he needed after all to go to Italy for personal business reasons, so could I take full ownership of the boat and business for just another £500. This hurried exit on his part was, I later discovered, in order to escape his creditors. But at the time his proposition seemed a bargain so I agreed when he told me he would meet me in Cannes to hand over the business. I duly transferred the money and sent a telegram to let him know when I would be coming by train from Paris a few days later. I packed hurriedly and set off for the Côte d'Azur. Of course when I got there he had gone, never to be seen again. To my relief the *Jane Mary* was still safely moored in the same berth. Black and his wife had obviously departed hurriedly, leaving even the beds unmade, but in every other respect the boat was shipshape.

I embraced the novelty of owning my own boat in the South of France and gradually got to know the fraternity of boat people, varying from successful skippers and experienced crews to handymen, itinerants and outright scroungers. But there was a dearth of work for the majority of boat people who lived around the harbour, although worthwhile jobs would occasionally come up. One sought-after job paying 50 francs per day was varnishing the tall masts of Errol Flynn's schooner by swinging from the topmasts in a bosun's chair. The picturesque old harbour at Cannes was packed with boats of all sizes and shapes moored two or three deep, so it was not unusual to be moving one's moorings to let others in and out, but it was well sheltered and conven-ient for the town, hotels, market and yacht chandlers. And port dues for small craft in the old harbour were negligible at that time. One walked everywhere barefoot, swam a lot and soon learned to live economically from the market: salade niçoise, baguettes, eggs and grapes were cheap and plentiful.

After checking out the engine, doing a little brass cleaning and deck scrub-bing, as well as checking the compass and charts, I was ready for my first foray out to the offshore island just a mile or two away, where one could anchor close inshore and stay at leisure for the day. This all seemed idyllic but I was going to need to earn some money.

It only remained to find some customers in order to pay my way. I had some cards printed and visited local hotels, offering to take people along the coast to Nice, Villefrance, Menton, Monte Carlo and San Remo. But with the season fast approaching its end and hot competition from other established boats I had little success until an ill-assorted group of three Greeks chartered the *Jane Mary* for a trip to Monaco and San Remo. They had their own nefarious reasons for wanting to visit these places. It was possible to load bonded goods such as cigarettes for travelling out of France to Monaco and Italy. Then, as it turned out later, they had plans to sell these goods in Italy. My passengers were not very good sailors and for my first charter voyage the weather turned rough. The boat, which had been in the water all summer, had a thick growth of weed on the hull so made only about 5 knots into the wind. Nonetheless we made it to Nice and then on to San Remo and Monte Carlo.

Monte Carlo, approached from the sea for the first time, was an unforgettable sight, with its elegant buildings ringing the harbour, and many grand motor yachts moored around against a background of pine tree-clad hills and, in the foreground, the azure-blue sea dotted with brilliant-white sails skimming in and out. Once tied up alongside I explored the town while my passengers went about their business, and we all had a good meal ashore

On my motor yacht *Jane Mary* in San Remo, 1965.

81

that evening. But during the night, while we slept aboard the *Jane Mary*, safely tied up at a pontoon, one of the passengers sloped off taking his companions' funds with him. The others, surprisingly, went to the police in the morning to report this theft of their possibly ill-gotten gains. Then with all their money gone the pair packed up and left, unfortunately unable even to pay me for the charter.

That evening, unshaven, because I had started to grow a beard during the voyage, and still dressed in my seagoing gear, I wandered disconsolately up towards the casino, where I was accosted by a smart policemen who demanded to see my passport. When I explained that I was the captain of a yacht in the harbour he clearly didn't believe me and took me down to the police station. It was a new experience for me to be taken into custody, but by now the *Jane Mary* was already known to the Monte Carlo police owing to the events of the previous night and I was courteously released.

The next day I had no alternative but to return to Cannes on my own with the boat, there to try unsuccessfully to get further charters before the season finally ended.

In September, after a very interesting and colourful few weeks, I concluded that there was nothing to be gained financially by spending the winter in Cannes. I arranged for a minder, a friendly Mexican rogue, to look after *Jane Mary*, which we moored alongside another larger boat that he was also tending. Then I set off for home. By bad judgement I took a train at Cannes for the journey to Paris on a Saturday night when it seemed half the French army were already on board and I had to prop myself with all my luggage in the corridor for twelve hours. Crossing the channel by the Newhaven ferry, I arrived home with mixed feelings but happy to see my family and get back to the real working world.

When I settled back at my parents' home, and after earning some pocket money picking apples for fruit growers in Suffolk, I offered my services temporarily to Royal Mail Lines who immediately suggested a job with a difference. This was to travel as the company's representative or 'Supercargo' on board a Bank Line motor ship, *Rowanbank*, chartered by Royal Mail to deliver general cargo to the West Indies. My copy of the *Time Charter*, now yellowed with age, shows that the 6308-gt *Rowanbank* was hired at a rate of £485 per day. The document states that the Supercargo is to 'see that the voyages are prosecuted with the utmost despatch ... He is to be furnished with free accommodation and same fare as provided for the Captain's table.' In practice, it was my job to contact the agents in each port, to order the gangs of stevedores when required, and to see that all the cargo was properly discharged, as well as to bear witness to any events that might lead to insurance claims on the cargo.

Bank Line was a large, well-established and respected tramp shipping line, whose cargo ships were manned by British deck officers with mainly Lascar crews. They were accustomed to visiting the South Sea islands and the officers had exotic tales to tell of their generous welcome from the Queen of Tonga herself when they dropped anchor there. The food on board *Rowanbank* was quite different from that in Royal Mail; the Lascar cooks regularly served up the most delicious curries that I've ever had and with all the trimmings.

But alas, we did not go to the South Seas on this trip. We simply went to the West Indies with general cargo calling in at Bermuda, Dominica and Haiti. The island encompassing Dominica and the Black Republic of Haiti appeared particularly poor and very unsophisticated. At Santo Domingo in Dominica I remember seeing gangs of large, strong and entirely naked men working on the sugar plantations. In the main square of Port-au-Prince, Haiti's capital, I visited the Cathedral and an art gallery where I was struck by the very primitive but highly colourful paintings; in retrospect I wish I had bought one of these inexpensive local exhibits of a type which later became so fashionable. We completed discharging our Royal Mail cargo in Montego Bay on the island of Jamaica, where I said my goodbyes to the crew of the *Rowanbank* and flew home, via Kingston, just before Christmas 1965. This concluded ten years of service with Royal Mail.

Thereafter I sought steady work for the rest of the winter with Blue Star Line until such time as I should return to the South of France and my boat. Blue Star, owned by Lord Vestey's group, ran meat-carrying ships from South America and Australasia and always had ships in London's Royal Docks. Shipping lines regularly required relieving staff to man their ships while in home ports, and between ports while their own ship's officers would be on leave. So in January 1966 I joined the *Caledonia Star* as Second Mate in the Victoria Dock and sailed with her round to Liverpool, before going straight across to Hull to bring the *Auckland Star* back to London. My Discharge Book reminds me that I coasted on three other Blue Star liners until the end of April 1966 when, having saved some cash by living on board these ships, it was time to return to France and get my boat ready for the season.

10

Yacht Delivery to the Mediterranean

I returned to Cannes in the spring of 1966, and had *Jane Mary* winched onto the quay and her hull cleaned and repainted, doing as much of this work as I could myself. I realised, however, that I would never be able to do more than scrape a living with the boat owing to the brevity of the high season for chartering, which was from mid July to mid September. In addition, the intense competition and expenses of keeping and maintaining my boat through the winter had to be reviewed.

So while living aboard *Jane Mary*, now back in the water, and looking for any opportune charters, I decided, with a thought to the future, to take advantage of the latest opening to further my nautical career by studying for a university degree. While working on ships in London during the winter, I had learnt of a new degree course in Maritime Sciences for certificated Master Mariners which was to be introduced at the University of Wales Institute of Science and Technology (UWIST). This course could be focused on either shipping business studies or technical and scientific studies. The latter, for which I opted, included basic maths and physics, meteorology and oceanology, ship control systems and naval architecture. It was necessary to do a correspondence course in A level science subjects prior to being accepted for this course due to begin in September that year; so, with some difficulty owing to all the distractions of summer in the South of France, I got stuck into this as best I could. Meanwhile I put *Jane Mary* up for sale again, not without some regrets at the prospect of losing such a very sound boat of a type rapidly becoming a classic rarity in the new age of plastic boat construction.

Meanwhile, as there were few sailors with any deep-sea navigation qualifications among those living and working on boats around the old harbour in Cannes, I was offered a job as navigator on a delivery voyage from England to Cannes in May that year. There being no remunerative charter work for the *Jane Mary* on the horizon, I gladly accepted this oppor-

The trimaran *L'Aroyo*.

tunity. There were to be three of us, including an experienced and very practical but academically unqualified sailing skipper and an ex-marine engineer, both of whom had been working on boats in Cannes for some time. The boat to be delivered was a brand-new Prout design 30-foot trimaran named *L'Aroyo* from Cox Marine in Lowestoft. This we had to collect from Great Yarmouth for its proud new owner, a restaurateur from Paris who had acquired a mooring in the old harbour of Antibes.

Built of marine ply, with a wide beam of about 20 feet across the three hulls, *L'Aroyo* had spacious accommodation in the large central hull with generous headroom and four berths. There was also a smaller double cabin to the rear of the cockpit. The broad beam allowed plenty of deck space, which was one of the attractions of this design. The two outer hulls, designed to provide buoyancy and stability along with speed, held water tanks and provided some storage space. In addition to the mainmast, which was stepped in a collar on deck, there was a mizzen mast set at the rear of the cockpit. So, we had a ketch rig with choice of jib, genoa or storm jib forward; mainsail with manual reefing; and smaller sail on the mizzen. For power we had only a 25-hp Crescent outboard motor set in a well aft. This was capable of giving us 4 knots but, with a 2,000-mile voyage ahead, and limited fuel space, the engine would be used only for manoeuvring in harbour and for emergencies.

Delivery crew of *L'Aroyo*, our skipper, Alan left.

Lightly built pleasure yachts would normally expect to take the Canal du Midi through France but our trimaran was too broad in the beam for this, so we had no choice but to brave the Atlantic weather. Our 2,000-mile voyage was to take us westward down the English Channel, round Ushant, south across the Bay of Biscay and along the Iberian Peninsular to Gibraltar, then through the western Mediterranean via the Balearics to Cannes.

Early that June, we set sail and had to beat down the Channel for a whole week against strong westerly winds. This was not the easiest of tasks in the three-hulled *L'Aroyo*, which would not sail closer than five points off the wind. Making broad tacks across the Channel we called in first at Newhaven for stores; there, too, it was nice to meet some of my sister's family who came to say goodbye. At the chandler's in Newhaven I selected charts of the Channel, Western Approaches, Biscay and western Mediterranean, although subsequent unexpected events were to show that we could have benefited from larger-scale Mediterranean charts with more detail of harbour approaches. I also acquired a compact Japanese radio direction finder which, in the absence of any other electronic navigational equipment, such as Decca or a radio telephone, was to prove invaluable. I brought with me my sextant, inherited from my uncle, which had been my regular tool of the trade while navigating passenger and cargo liners. It was to prove much harder to use low down on the heaving deck of a small and very wet boat, but nonetheless it was eventually to save us from possible disaster.

Benefiting from an onshore wind we sailed smoothly along the south coast for a while, and as we passed Brighton Pier were rewarded by catching two mackerel from a line which we kept streamed astern. These were to be the only fish we caught throughout the voyage, although our spinner and line were later taken by some large fish or possibly a porpoise off the Portuguese coast.

Our next tack took us across the Channel to Cherbourg where, since we would be entirely reliant on the magnetic compass and I was anxious to check this for errors, we were fortuitously able to put a bowline onto a buoy in the large military harbour basin early one morning. With our charted position and transit bearings of various landmarks I could 'swing the compass' following the theory taught at nautical college. This allowed me to draw up a sufficiently accurate table of deviations from true bearings of the magnetic compass as we swung the boat on her engine in a circle through all the points of the compass. It was not long, however, before an irate French-speaking Morse lamp ordered us away. Having completed our task, we were able to beat a hasty retreat before the guns were rolled out, and we resumed our voyage. With a particularly stubborn force 5–6 headwind we battled back across the Channel on a tack which was of necessity just too broad to allow us to clear Portland Bill. So we fell foul of the tide race off the Bill, my first experience of this notorious yachtsman's hazard. We found ourselves surrounded by breaking peaks of water towering above us, and were unable to maintain a steady course or keep wind in the sails, while we were swept ever closer inshore. By heading into the wind with engine on full throttle we battled on, being driven meanwhile inshore by waves and current, until quite suddenly at only about two hundred yards from this unfriendly short stretch of coastline, we found ourselves in relatively calm waters and able to resume our westward progress.

Thence we sailed to Falmouth for a short rest and the serious business of taking on fuel, water and bonded stores for our voyage to the Mediterranean. Two days later we set off, taking advantage of moderate westerly winds, which allowed us to make a quick crossing to Ushant. The three of us kept regular watches, alternating on the wheel day and night. Alan, our skipper, proved to be a natural 'boat person', looking after all the sailing gear and making repairs as we went along. He also organised the food so that by brewing up a meat and cabbage stew in a huge pot on the Calor gas stove and reheating this each day, with addition of more baked beans and curry powder as necessary, we were kept nourished through the days of heavy weather that followed.

As we turned south to cross the Bay of Biscay, the wind increased to gale force from the north-west. In no time alarmingly high waves built up and bore down on us from the starboard quarter, these rising some 20 feet above the hull, then lifting the stern as the crests passed under us. We ran on jib alone under the grey stormy sky, surfing down the waves in a way which was both thrilling and frightening; the rigging hummed and the whole hull vibrated under the strain. Surely *L'Aroyo* was not built to take this, but we were committed and had no choice but to run before the wind. In fact, we crossed the Bay in about forty-eight hours. It was a wonderful relief to see my dead reckoning and allowance for leeway justified, for we had no other means of navigating under these conditions, when, soon after dark on our third night out, we saw on the port bow the lights of Corunna and the northern Spanish coast.

I was a little alarmed, however, to discover one night just how bad was the bespectacled Alan's eyesight. As I came out to take over the helm he pointed out the lights of a 'fishing boat away to starboard'. In fact, this was a large passenger ship which crossed our bow close ahead, no doubt bound for Vigo. Bearing in mind that Bill, our engineer, had all along confessed to poor eyesight, I realised that I would have to be the eyes for all three of us.

Next day, as we crept slowly south under sail in the lightest of breezes and pleasant summer sunshine, Portuguese fishermen, who had materialised out of the dawn mist, came alongside and we exchanged some of our duty-free cigarettes and whisky for fresh fish and wine. I was able to take a noon sun sight to check our southerly progress. A day on which it was good to be at sea.

Then overnight calm and fog descended. Although the lights of several fishing vessels could be seen on the horizon there was a layer of thick fog above, and as we crept eerily at about 3 knots towards that gap between Cape Carvoeiro and outlying islands, signals from the Berlings radio beacon told me that the Berlings Islands were to starboard. The loud fog siren sounded almost directly above us as we passed within a mile of the island's cliffs, and we could even hear the surf on the beach, yet we saw no sign of the lighthouse due to the low blanket of fog, despite the light's nominal 32-mile range of visibility. That night I was very glad to have our portable direction finder, which confidently signalled that the Berlings beacon was passing safely down our starboard side.

Negotiating through the shipping traffic off Lisbon we worked our way down the coast and had a good westerly breeze on the starboard quarter when we rounded Cape St Vincente bound for Gibraltar. However, days of salt spray had taken their toll, corroding our electrics so that it became quite impossible to start the engine. It was thus that, under sail alone, Alan boldly tacked into the port of Gibraltar and we were able to moor for a hard-earned rest after eight days at sea.

After a two-day stay in Gibraltar for storing, although still unable to use the engine, we set sail again in the afternoon on our easterly course. On the very next day we were confronted by the levanter, a sharp easterly wind. As the weather deteriorated, this quickly churned up a short rough head sea, so that we shipped water continuously, and it was difficult to make any headway. Although we reduced sail, seas breaking over the bow stove in the perspex windows of our forward deckhouse and started to flood the cabin.

So we were in the unenviable position of bucking rough seas, with low scudding clouds, the wind now reaching gale force, out of sight of land, taking in water and having to pump the bilges manually. With darkness due to descend within a few hours, we had little choice but to head for shelter. The Spanish coast, east of Malaga, would, by dead reckoning, have been about ten miles north of us. The sun showed briefly in the west through the clouds for a few seconds at a time, so in desperation, propped against the mizzen on the heaving deck, I used my sextant to take a hasty sight under conditions that one would not normally dream of trusting. Using my watch, recently corrected by radio time signal, and the yachtsman's standard *Reeds Almanac* I calculated a position line which ran roughly north and south (i.e. at right angles to the sun in the west). This line passed directly through a dot on our small-scale Admiralty chart of the western Mediterranean which marked the fishing port of Adra; importantly this had a lighthouse on the headland.

With little knowledge of our emergency destination we headed north-wards, although our violently swinging compass could not give that accurate a course. Under those conditions, the sun sight could easily have been as much as five miles out, even assuming I had got my hasty observation and sums right, so in the gathering dusk as we sailed towards the unknown coast it was a tremendous relief to see the headland and lighthouse loom out of the gloom fine on our starboard bow. We sailed into a large bay as darkness fell, dropping anchor at the first available opportunity.

We all three slept very soundly that night, in fact too soundly for, in the storm which had been brewing, we dragged our anchor right across the harbour bay until it fouled that of a large store vessel close to the shore and there it held fast. However, we were safe and during the next day made friends with neighbouring boats who were amazed at our sudden appearance on the scene. After drying out we acquired the necessary wood – pieces of fish boxes given us by the fishermen – to board up the forward cabin ports and seal them. This being primarily a fishing port the locals were quick to introduce us to an excellent unsophisticated fish restaurant for a welcome relaxed evening. The next morning, with favourable weather, we were off again. Unfortunately we still had no luck with the engine, but we were able to sail out of the wide bay and round the headland as we turned east again for Ibiza.

Bill and Alan had contacts in Ibiza who, they hoped, would be able to make the necessary engine repairs, so we called in there. Bill went off to see about the engine repairs but was not very successful. The electrics were now too corroded and the engine itself would need a thorough overhaul. Meanwhile we had a pleasant 48-hour break, and were wined and dined by Alan's friends. Bill located a sunken semi-submerged ship's lifeboat which he believed could be renovated and arranged to buy this for £50, apparently having nursed for some time his own secret ambition to do up a motor boat in the Mediterranean.

So we sailed from Ibiza, bound at last for Cannes; we ran south of Majorca then on the second day out, taking advantage of a good north-westerly, tacked up between the islands of Majorca and Minorca. Land faded astern as we started to cross the Gulf of Lion, making good headway in a fresh breeze. Then at 0500 the next morning disaster struck. Alan, on watch, had already called me as the wind was getting more squally and we had been running on full sail with the main, mizzen and genoa.

We were just preparing to reduce sail in the early dawn, when a line squall hit us. A characteristic of these squalls is that, as one encounters a band of low cloud and rain, the wind strengthens and veers through up to 180 degrees. This it did, backing in the billowing genoa sail. The forestay snapped and the mast fell in a tangle of rigging into the sea. The noise of the wind and our motion through the water were suddenly replaced by an eerie silence as we wallowed dismasted. The line squall passed, the wind eased and we set systematically about disentangling the rigging and lashing the mast alongside in the grey light of early morning. As full daylight came we could see that the galvanised iron rigging screw at the base of the forestay had snapped, and that the all-too-weak 2-inch high steel collar on deck, in which the mast was stepped in this type of trimaran, had been bent so releasing the mast, though the mast itself was undamaged. The small mizzen sail, while useful for balance and steering was on its own unable to give us headway. However, Alan's experience was invaluable in enabling us to set up a jury rig, using the jib sail suspended from the mast's boom stepped in the damaged mainsail collar. This jury mast was held vertical by four guy ropes which we led forward and aft from the boom head to the gunwales on either side.

Being roughly equidistant from the Balearics and the French coast, which was some 100 miles away, we were barely manoeuvrable and would be at the mercy of the elements. Should we fail to make headway and run out of stores and water we were prepared to call for assistance from any passing ship. I had the Morse lamp ready and manufactured a distress flag – the code flag X, which is a red St Andrew's cross on a white background. For this an old sheet with a roughly stitched cross made of red bunting had to suffice.

The elements were, however, kind to us from now on. As the wind had steadied from the north-west, about force 5, we were actually able to limp along at about 2 knots in our intended direction towards the French coast. And when a tanker crossed our bow we gave no further thought to calling for assistance. Though to the tanker, *L'Aroyo*, dismasted with the cabin front boarded up, must have looked very much like another *Kon-Tiki* raft.

Luck was with us and the wind held. So it was that we sighted the Côte d'Azur and late on a Saturday night we drifted into the harbour at Cannes, where we tied up at the first available berth. This, fortuitously, was a repair berth on the west side of the port. We fell fast asleep, but were awoken about 0600 on Sunday morning by a tirade of shouting to the effect that we had no business to be there and must go away – *vite*! It was not difficult to show, even with our modest command of the French language, that this was impossible; we had no means of moving, but perhaps, with their magnificent crane, they would be kind enough to put our mast back up for us. This they did with surprising ease and we were able to fix the mast collar and secure the rigging with new rigging screws. The only thing then was to replace the cabin front windows, applying a bit of mastic and paint here and there. When all this was done Alan went ashore to telephone the owner, Monsieur Gerrard, who was at his summer apartment in Antibes. He was immeasurably relieved to hear from us after six weeks of silence and came down to see *L'Aroyo* that evening in high spirits. Bill arranged to depart the very next day, his heart still being with the sunken lifeboat in Ibiza, while Alan and I stayed to get the engine overhauled ashore and then sailed round to Antibes where Monsieur Gerrard had arranged a permanent mooring buoy for us. There Alan, his job done, also said goodbye. He had taught me a lot about sailing under all conceivable conditions; I had got to know the boat well and when invited to stay on as skipper for the rest of the season I was only to happy to do so.

I had a wonderful few weeks looking after *L'Aroyo* at her mooring in Antibes. My chief duties were to keep the boat clean, deal with boat chandlers for any necessities or problems during the week and have the icebox full with the Gerrard's favourite rosé wine by the weekend when he and his wife would come down from Paris. We were then free to sail out to the islands for picnicking and swimming or go further afield to such harbours as Villefranche to the east or St Tropez to the west.

I also now had an offer to buy the *Jane Mary,* which had become a bit of a financial worry. I therefore sold up for what now seems a ridiculously cheap sum, barely half my initial payment, an investment that might have paid well enough if I had been able to keep her. That was, however, out of the question. The port authorities soon tightened up on harbour dues for a start, and today one has to be a very rich man to keep a boat in the Port of Cannes. I had, however, learnt a lesson from my adventures in Cannes and have never trusted any apparently wonderful business ventures since. The more window dressing, such as magnificent lunches in luxurious surroundings, the less such 'opportunities' should be trusted. The good news was that, as well as having made good contacts and friends in the South of France and learnt a lot about sailing, I had been accepted to start my new studies at UWIST in Cardiff that autumn term.

11

My Time at UWIST, Cardiff

Students digs in Cardiff that winter were a bit of a shock after the benign climate and dazzling holiday atmosphere of the Côte d'Azur. However, with the novelty of being a student in the Maritime Department morale was high among the twelve of us mature students, all from different shipping companies; we were guinea pigs for a new academic course, and would have to live on small grants of £11 a week. We also had to work hard in the first place just to catch up with other A level students, particularly in our maths which at sea had been specifically directed towards spherical trigonometry for navigation over the Earth's surface and unconcerned with such intricacies as calculus. In addition, the specialist subjects we had to study were still evolving at the time; for example, ship control systems encompassed the theory of advanced autopilots which anticipated ship movements and new types of radar display to include collision avoidance and radar plotting aids (ARPA), while ship construction was entering the new era of very large tankers, heavy bulk carriers and large container ships. It was also becoming quite common to 'jumboise' a ship, that is, to increase its length by welding in a complete new midsection, in order to gain the economic advantages of scale. This, of course gave our enthusiastic young tutor in naval architecture wonderful opportunities to tie us up in knots over all the questions of stresses, stability, weight, powering and speed that become involved in such engineering as splitting a ship's hull and towing hull sections to other docks for joining.

On the whole we enjoyed college life and the novel situation of having a good deal more experience of the world, if not academic expertise, than some of our lecturers. During our time in the Maritime Department at UWIST, the Nautical Institute was formed in order to provide a professional body for ships' officers, to set standards for the science and safety of ship operations, and to establish codes of conduct for shipowners and operators. Objectives included 'promoting a high standard of qualification, competence and knowledge among those in control of seagoing craft'. At that time to qualify as a full member one had to be a Master Mariner, and most of our class did in fact join the Nautical Institute as founder members. Largely under the guidance of the Secretary, Julian Parker, an ex-P&O officer, the Institute grew and flourished, broadened the scope of its membership, held many seminars and over the ensuing years played an important role in setting standards and influencing legislation on ship safety.

Our attempts to compete on the sports field with other departments at UWIST were fun but laughable. The Engineering Department in particular were good rugby players as was only to be expected in Wales and they trounced us, which was not surprising as we had not been in training; we even found it necessary to sit down with bottles of beer to get our breath back at half-time. I also took up dinghy sailing with the college club. In years at sea I had only once had the leisure time to go dinghy sailing, that with the Yacht Club in Buenos Aires. Cardiff Docks was a very different kettle of fish. I remember capsizing in the filthy water and trying for days to get the coal dust out of my socks.

One traditional event was a raft race between all the departments at UWIST. In the winter that I took part, the race was held on a February morning, a particularly cold and frosty one at that. The course ran down the swift-flowing river Taff from Taffs-Well over about 6 miles of shallows and rapids of dirty water to the bridge in the centre of Cardiff. We in the Maritime Department had to build our own raft for a crew of five. I suppose being nautical we should have done well, but we didn't. Others with local knowledge knew better what was required and the winning raft was constructed of rubber tyres well lashed together so that, being pliable, it could bump its way over the stones. Our raft, a catamaran arrangement of wooden platform on oil drums did well enough until we hit the shallows when it simply broke up on the stones, leaving us floundering in the icy water. A long walk along the riverbank then followed, during which I had the odd sensation of feeling completely numb from the waist down. On finally making our way to the road, our sodden crew were able to get lifts back to town.

Watching the rugby at Cardiff Arms Park was one of our most favoured pastimes. The whole city was enthused by the internationals, but we always managed to find standing room somehow. Then there was the School of Music and Drama situated in the old Castle buildings, giving us the opportunity to mingle socially and offering more cultured entertainment. There were also some very nice pubs in the countryside a few miles away to drive to at weekends or in the summer evenings. After years at sea this student life was all a great novelty.

Above all, it was a delight to look forward to long summer vacations and for my first I could not resist going back to Antibes with its old walled town and harbour, there to spend a couple of months. I had met and made friends with a charming couple, Michael and Ann Bridgman, while in Antibes with *L'Aroyo* the previous summer. Ann ran a jewellery and craft shop in the medieval village of Biot a few miles away in the hills above Cannes while Michael acted part-time as an agent for Hurley Marine. In the port they kept a very neat three-berth Hurley 21-foot GRP demonstration sailing boat, which was equipped with an outboard motor housed in a well aft. I had been out sailing with the Bridgmans on fine days the previous summer and I was now able to live on board for my vacation, looking after the boat and demonstrating it to anyone who might be interested. Not that we ever did secure any sales, but I found the boat very easy to handle and sail on my own, and just the right size to carry a couple of passengers. I did once or twice take a diving instructor from the Casino at Cannes out sailing in exchange for some instruction with diving gear in the Casino pool, but decided to stick to snorkelling as I was never particularly happy with air bottles, the pressure always giving me lasting headaches at any depth.

The Côte d'Azur is very much tuned to fair-weather sailing; the wind is usually gentle, often too gentle, and there are no tides to worry about. But everyone's fear is the mistral, a near-gale-force northerly wind which can blow for two or three days at a time. When this is forecast there is hardly a boat to be seen out at sea, however balmy the weather may actually be.

So I passed a pleasant summer in 1967, getting to know many other boat people, learning to snorkel for sea urchins – one eats raw the eggs of the brown female sea urchins dug out of their spiky shells – and to catch small shrimps to eat raw from among the pontoon fenders. Another more sophisticated pastime for those with fast motor yachts is to go fishing for tuna. This is best done on a calm day, when one can look out for the turbulence on the sea surface, and for excited seabirds which all congregate in the spot where tuna are feeding off shoals of small fish. The trick is for the motor boat to head directly towards the area at about 24 knots, and then slow down to glide through the shoal trailing spinners. I enjoyed being invited to go along for this exhilarating sport but have to say I was never present when any tuna were caught.

Then it was time to go back to Cardiff for another year's study.

12

Delivering a Patrol Vessel to South-West Africa

For the summer break before my last year at UWIST in Cardiff, I signed on as Chief Officer for one final trip under the Red Ensign, and this was the most bizarre of all my voyages to date. I had already enjoyed two very pleasant summer vacations in the South of France looking after the trimaran and the Hurley 22 in Antibes, but this time I was looking for something different, and preferably an occupation which would pay me a bit of money.

Towards the end of term I had seen an advertisement in the *South Wales Echo* for officers and crew required to deliver a patrol vessel to South-West Africa; the departure date and expected month's voyage fitted in very neatly so I duly answered the box number and was interviewed in Cardiff by the prospective master. I learnt that Captain Wills had been at sea in Esso tankers in the 1950s, but had retired with poor eyesight, then emigrated to South-West Africa, where he worked as a port officer in Walvis Bay; he was a well-respected citizen and had recently been the Mayor of that town. So when the South-West African fishery protection service wanted an offshore patrol vessel to counteract smuggling and illegal fishing they duly selected Bill Wills to come to England to purchase and deliver a second-hand vessel. They must have given him a very limited budget – I never did discover exactly how much he paid for the vessel – but the contract was negotiated with a car dealer in Swansea, and a Second World War US minesweeper *William R*, of 245 gross tons, was duly purchased.

The *William R* was a 'Mickey Mouse' coastal minesweeper, a class so named because of the big round portholes like eyes on the forward bulkhead of the wheelhouse. She was about 120ft long, built entirely of wood as was the custom, this having been the best material for vessels engaged in mine warfare before the advent of GRP and anti-magnetic steel. The hull was solid enough oak, but bearing in mind that these ships had been built in a great hurry during the war some twenty-four years earlier, it was hardly surprising that by now the laminated wood superstructure was in poor condition. Both the engines (two original General Motors diesels which were supposed to give speeds of 12 knots) and the deck machinery were in very bad repair, but a marine engineering and vehicle repair company from Newport gave the machinery an overhaul. Somehow the *William R* acquired a certificate of seaworthiness and we crew were duly signed on at Newport on the 1st July 1968, the last of the fifty-five recorded voyages in my Discharge Book.

On paper we were a well-qualified crew for we three watchkeepers, the Captain, myself and Alan Simpson the Second Mate, all had Master's Certificates, although the Captain's vision was distinctly questionable and the elderly, though experienced, Second Mate had, we believed, been dismissed from the Royal Fleet Auxiliary for being over-attached to the bottle, while I was now a somewhat rusty mature student rather than a regular seagoing officer.

So we put to sea, with our Captain who had not been to sea for fifteen years, myself as Chief Officer, a disgruntled but now sober Second Mate, a quick-tempered Jamaican cook recruited from the docks, two car mechanics without any seagoing experience as ship's engineers, and two black African deckhands whose aim was to get back to their homelands but who, unfortunately, belonged to two rival tribes that did not care to mix.

The patrol boat *William R* at Las Palmas for engine repairs en route for South West Africa. *(Author's photo 1968)*

100

Our destination was Walvis Bay, with a scheduled stop at Las Palmas in the Canaries where we would take on more diesel fuel, as the *William R* did not have the range to get us there directly. Our first three days at sea were relatively uneventful, though we were unable to do more than 11 knots with a fair wind, and our old minesweeper was an uncomfortable ride in any sort of swell such as we experienced across Biscay. The ship was fitted with one of the earliest and crudest form of autopilots; sensors on the magnetic compass directed a signal to turn a cog and chain, just like a bicycle chain, on the spindle of the steering wheel, thus turning the rudder to bring the ship's head back towards the course originally set. So, with the turning of a cranking chain, the unmanned wheel would be spinning continuously one way or the other. This was passably acceptable in fair weather away from land but one of the deckhands would have to steer manually in rough weather as well as whenever manoeuvring in coastal waters and when approaching port.

Then, one afternoon, there was a loud bang, followed by billows of smoke from the engine room, and we were down to one engine. We limped on to Las Palmas where we anchored safely in the large harbour area which has the advantage of being well protected by a mile-long curved breakwater. A survey of the damage showed that some new parts would be required including a set of piston rings. These could only be obtained from the United States and telegrams were duly exchanged; meanwhile there was little we could do except wait. It was pleasant weather and a safe enough anchorage so I decided to take the opportunity to paint the ship up along with the two deckhands, using the store of paint on board. We painted the bridge and accommodation block in battleship grey, overside in black and, wearing life jackets and leaning over from the ship's boat, a neat white waterline. We did make the old relic look quite a tidy picture, at least outwardly.

Meanwhile there was plenty of time to exchange news with our various neighbours at anchor. In all my time with the Royal Mail A-boats, when we had been too busy loading and discharging mail and cargo during our few hours stay at Las Palmas ever to walk beyond the breakwater, I had never previously met up with other inhabitants of the port or realised what a crossroads for passing ships and boats this island was. Ships and boats converged on voyages between northern Europe, the Mediterranean, West Africa, the West Indies and the Americas.

There was one 30-foot sailing yacht from the UK with father and daughter on board; they were emigrating to New Zealand but waiting for the hurricane season to pass before heading across the Atlantic to the West Indies en route for Panama. Mother had sensibly gone on by ship with the furniture. Then there were three young men in a converted lifeboat from somewhere in the Mediterranean who had picked up a hitchhiking Polish girl in Gibraltar; they were heading for Liberia with the intention of opening a night club there. Consumed with curiosity about other voyagers, I rowed over to an 18-foot folkboat with two Danes on board; these lads were on a pilgrimage to America to visit John Kennedy's grave. I hardly believed this until I saw all the memorabilia of JFK around the cabin.

One day a sturdy Shetland fishing boat chugged in and anchored nearby. Three Scots lads had bought this boat to sail to Cape Town; quite an undertaking because none of them had ever been deep sea before, nor did they have any navigation equipment other than an atlas, the boat compass and a hand bearing compass; they told me they preferred not to get out of sight of land! I brought them to look at my charts and we agreed their best courses through the Cape Verde Islands and round Gambia. It turned out that they were scuba diving enthusiasts and had been subsisting on the fish which they harpooned. I was delighted when they invited me to have a go and instructed me carefully, anchored there in the harbour, but alas I found that 20 feet down was about my limit for I developed such a headache that lasted for all of the next two days. I knew then that I could never be a diver, much as I was fascinated by the underwater world, but that I would have to restrict myself to snorkelling. These lads then set off for Cape Town with the intention of selling their boat and buying a Land Rover which they would drive up through Africa and home to Scotland. I never heard any more of them but such was their optimism, resourcefulness and the seaworthiness of their boat that I've no doubt they made it.

When our precious parcels of engine parts were eventually flown out to Las Palmas, our engines were duly repaired with the assistance of marine engineers ashore. *William R* did engine trials and then went alongside to load barrels of fuel oil, which we stowed on the afterdeck, sufficient to fuel our engines through the 4,000-mile run to Walvis Bay that still lay ahead of us. We needed more stores too; our fare was pretty basic and the sausages were already going off though the cook refused to admit it. I am more than a little surprised there were no cases of food poisoning on board.

We had now been in Las Palmas for a full month and all hands were glad to be off again in early August. Having crossed the Equator southward passing through the doldrums and south-east trades, we then encountered some stormy weather and a steep swell which had us rolling and pitching heavily so that the screws raced each time the stern lifted, and our speed made good was reduced to about 7 knots. There was one alarm when our drums of fuel, which were stood upright on the heaving afterdeck, worked loose in their wire lashings but we survived this potential crisis until calmer weather allowed us to secure the remaining drums. On another occasion, while bucketing in heavy seas, our electronic depth sounder simply fell off the wheelhouse bulkhead due to the rottenness of the wood structure.

Very wearily we docked at Walvis Bay at about midnight on 26th August, a whole month later than originally intended. Immediately the port police boarded the ship, unable to conceal their impatience and, without a word of thanks, ordered us to disembark the next morning. They made no secret of the fact that the *William R*, with her lack of speed and doubtful sea-worthiness, was a disappointment. Unceremoniously, we crew split up to go our separate ways. I had hoped to enjoy a week or two in Africa, possibly going up to see the Victoria Falls, but because our voyage had been so prolonged it was time to head straight home to prepare for my last year at college. So from the dry and dusty Walvis Bay, my only view of the lands and wildlife of South-West Africa was while winding up in the steam train through the national park to Windhoek where Alan Simpson and I took a plane to London.

13

Becoming a Maritime Journalist

Back in Cardiff, I passed out B.Sc. (Hons) without any great distinction at UWIST in the summer of 1969. Nonetheless, as the first pioneering class of Master Mariners taking the new Maritime Studies degree course we were as well qualified as possible academically in the nautical profession. So what were our future prospects? Some went back to their old shipping companies in positions of management, one or two back to sea, and some into nautical education; one, John King, the most distinguished academically of our class, stayed on to lecture and was soon to become a professor at UWIST.

For my part, having studied naval architecture and incidentally written a thesis on developments in the design of container ships, I applied to and was elected a member of the Royal Institution of Naval Architects. Although I had no clear idea of what I should do when I left Cardiff, I was, as the end of our last term approached in the summer of 1969, tempted by a newspaper advertisement for a consultant naval architect required to join the editorial team of the *The Motor Ship*. This was a monthly technical trade journal belonging to the IPC group, a journal which had the reputation of being the best in its field and, well supported by advertising, the fattest. *The Motor Ship*, founded between the wars when motor ships first became established, had in fact broadened its horizons to cover all aspects of ship design, construction, marine engineering and outfitting of coastal and deep-sea shipping. So when new types of ship were delivered or seminars were held on their design it was *The Motor Ship*'s job to report in detail.

Following an interview with Bill Wilson, the Editor, himself a former seagoing engineer, I was welcomed to join the team at IPC's office in Farringdon Street, London, which was the headquarters of its marine and technical journals. Three other members of the editorial team were ex-seagoing engineers and to be working alongside other ex-seafarers immediately made me feel more at home in this final break from my seagoing career.

Also I was very quickly sent off to cover the design features of new ships as they were delivered, to attend sea trials or make short voyages in them when possible. I was able, also, to see the latest developments at shipyards, where drydocks, covered shipbuilding and prefabrication halls were starting to take the place of conventional slipway launching methods.

My first assignment was a cross-Channel trip in the *Vortigern,* a passenger and car ferry built by British Shipbuilders in 1969 for the British Rail/Sealink service. The report I submitted on her hull design, layout, machinery, accommodation, navigational and cargo facilities, ran to over 3,000 words. The Editor put great store in reference to the names of as many manufacturers as possible, for this was to be an incentive to advertisers who provided the journal's main source of income. My report was well received and published in full; so it seemed I had qualified as a journalist, thereby joining a small close-knit maritime technical group in the UK writing for magazines and trade journals. We got to know pretty well everyone in our field, all of us with a common interest in ships and the sea.

Early on I enjoyed a delightful journalists' 'jolly' with the Danish shipping company DFDS, first crossing from Harwich to Esbjerg by the fine ferry *Winston Churchill,* taking a local car ferry to Copenhagen, then going round to the northern shipbuilding town of Aalborg to see a brand-new car and passenger ship named the *Aalborg,* and returning cross-country to Esbjerg to join another ship home. Throughout this trip we were wined and dined royally by our hosts, but there's no free lunch and on returning home detailed technical descriptions and plans of the various ships were expected for publication within days.

At this time great strides forward were being made in the design of new roll-on roll-off car and passenger ferries. These were fitted with bow and stern doors so that vehicles could drive through, a novelty in deep-sea vessels at the time but common enough now; the ships were stabilised for comfort and took advantage of new lightweight easily cleaned materials for outfitting public rooms and cabins.

Also at this time we were experiencing the evolution of the supertanker, initially up to 250,000 tons deadweight, first developed around 1967, and bulk carriers reaching sizes up to 150,000 tons – an evolution never dreamt of a decade earlier. Meanwhile larger-than-ever container ships were being designed and shore terminals built to receive them, a revolution which was to change fundamentally the carriage of dry cargo by sea.

So there was plenty to keep up with. This was an interesting life but hard work as, in addition to travelling to shipyards and ships, our editorial copy had to be ready for each monthly deadline, and this at a time before we had any word processors to assist our output of copy. One had also to learn the technicalities of proof-reading, setting copy and cutting and pasting the columns of print by hand, to make up pages of one's own articles to fit the designated space available.

After I had been working for IPC for about fifteen months, the Royal Institution of Naval Architects (RINA) advertised for an editor to start a new house journal. Previously, that is for about a hundred years, this learned society had produced four quarterly volumes of Transactions which were verbatim reports on lectures and technical reports by eminent naval architects and engineers, complete with their ensuing discussions, thus providing a unique record of the evolution and development of ship design over more than a century.

RINA had been founded in 1860 from its earlier roots in the Society for the Improvement in Naval Architecture, out of which the Royal Corps of Naval Constructors (RCNC) had also evolved. The original Society was founded in 1791 by a bookseller, Sewell, who was convinced of the superiority of French warship design at the time; he published collected papers of the Society in 1800. The most famous works of the early Society were a series of model tests on the stability and resistance of various ship forms in which Colonel Beaufoy carried out tests in Greenland Dock, London, between 1793 and 1798 using models up to 42ft long. The problem of estimating the resistance of full-size ships was finally solved by William Froude some seventy years later.

Now RINA intended to produce more immediate news on ship design and construction, along with the technical papers which were being produced regularly for discussion at meetings. I applied successfully for the job of Editor at the RINA's headquarters, a Georgian house on the Belgravia Estate, and started work there, at the age of thirty-eight, in January 1971. I suppose you could say this was the height of my career.

It was certainly a challenging enough start. My first quarterly journal was to be produced by April and I was lucky enough to have the help of just one secretary, Libby Sheldon, a charming girl whom I recruited from my parents' home village of Lamarsh in Suffolk. She was the first of several editorial secretaries I had working for me over the years that followed, though most chose, understandably, to move on to less technically specialised and more artistic or glamorous fields of publishing.

After much discussion with the Publications Committee we had agreed, perhaps not very imaginatively, that the journal's title should be *The Naval Architect*, but the title has survived to this day as the journal, now monthly, has become recognised as probably the world's leading journal in its field.

To take on full responsibility for the production of this journal, which was to serve the world's ship designers and marine engineers, was a daunting task. I did, however, have steadfast support from the Secretary of the Institution, Peter Ayling and was greatly encouraged by the President of RINA, Sir Alfred Sims KCB, RCNC, formerly Director General of Ships for the Ministry of Defence. Moral support also came from members of the RINA Council who had taken the initiative in establishing a journal, including its chairman, Alec Silverleaf, and other well-known naval architects such as A.N. Harrison CB, James Paffett of the National Physical Laboratory, D.K. Brown RCNC, a great historian, and Marshall Meek, senior naval architect for Blue Funnel and designer of the new generation of Overseas Container Line (OCL) fleet of container ships which were just then coming into service.

However, no sooner were we to get down to the business of producing the first journal than there ensued a postal strike which lasted for several weeks. This was a serious worry as at that time there were no fax machines or e-mails to simplify communications. The budget required that we should acquire some revenue through advertising, so, in addition to writing copy and soliciting articles, I had to cajole companies into placing advertisements in a still unseen journal – I did manage to get ten though for that first issue. Then there was the production side of publishing the journal, delivering copy to our chosen printers, Unwins of Woking, setting the pages by the traditional cut-and-paste method and proof-reading every word, again with the able help of my secretary. All was well, however, and in April 1971 we produced 7,000 copies of the first RINA journal which to my great relief was well received by the Council. For the first issue I chose to display the Institution's magnificent crest in full colour on the front cover. This crest carries the inscription 'Salum et Carinae Pignora Vitae', which translates as 'To the open sea and keel of a ship we pledge our lives'.

In July of that first year I was lucky to be able to go with Sir Alfred Sims and officials of RINA to Lisbon as guests of the Portuguese institution Ordem dos Engenheiros, where we were royally entertained, even meeting the President of Portugal. We attended joint society technical meetings, and visited shipyards including the mighty Lisnave shipyard; this had a new drydock specifically designed to build the latest type of VLCC supertankers of 250,000 tonnes capacity.

At that time, with the doubling of oil imports to north-west Europe over the previous eight years, very large crude carriers (VLCCs) were coming into their own and naval architects had successfully faced the structural challenges of size, weight and volume in construction; indeed two tankers of 477,000 tonnes deadweight capacity had just been ordered from Japan, as big as any we see plying the oceans today. There were serious design considerations for a million-ton crude-oil tanker (this would have been equivalent in capacity to sixteen T2 tankers like my old *Stanwell*), which although technically feasible with regard to structure, propulsion and manoeuvrability, never came to fruition due to the changing economic situation. In fact, the largest tanker in service today is about 564,000 tonnes. More ambitious projects of the early 1970s such as giant submarine oil tankers, oceangoing air-cushion vehicles or vast hovercraft failed to materialise.

Meanwhile, the sea transport of liquefied natural gas (LNG) and liquid petroleum gas (LPG) was, in the early 1970s, a relatively new industry for which the technology was fast developing, involving high pressures and exceedingly low cargo temperatures to keep the gas liquefied in cylindrical or spherical tanks. Larger and more sophisticated gas carrier fleets were to grow rapidly over the next decade.

Oil exploration was escalating in the North Sea and elsewhere, so that a new breed of offshore vessels, drill ships, semi-submersible drilling rigs and fixed platforms were being designed and built, bringing a new dimension of marine engineering to supplement traditional ship design and cloud the divisions between the two.

In 1971 nuclear propulsion for merchant ships was at the prototype stage; the first German ship, the 14,000-dwt cargo ship *Otto Hahn*, with a pressurised water reactor, had entered service in 1968 and now the fourth, the 8200-dwt *Mutsu*, was newly built in Japan. However, nuclear-powered merchant ships failed to gain general acceptance. Studies around 1974 for nuclear-powered German 80,000-dwt containerships and US 600,000-dwt tankers also came to naught due to the economics of construction. Nuclear ships were very expensive to build, maintenance was a worry and some countries, such as New Zealand, would not permit them in their ports, so this technology was soon abandoned for all but a few specialised ship types such as icebreakers and naval ships.

Then there was the revolution of large container shipping as a means of transporting goods worldwide. Although British designers and shipping companies were in the forefront of this, the ships themselves were too big to be built in British shipyards. Container ships have continued to grow in size, to some four times the capacity of those original Liverpool Bay class – which could themselves carry 2,300 20ft containers – about which I wrote in April 1971.

In fact, British shipbuilding, once a proud tradition in Belfast, on the Clyde and on Tyneside, was already shrinking rapidly by 1971. Britain's

The cargo ship *Bencruachan* under tow to Durban after her entire bow section was buckled by a freak wave off the South African coast. (*The Naval Architect*, July 1975)

proportion of world shipbuilding had declined from 50 per cent just after the war to just 10 per cent in 1966. Elsewhere, in Scandinavia particularly, there was large investment in covered shipbuilding yards, with which we could not compete, nor could we compete with the economics of building in Japan, which became the new world leader in ship construction.

Naval architects traditionally tested out the behaviour of different hull forms afloat in varying sea conditions and reported on these findings in technical papers within our journal. Research establishments, such as Admiralty Experiment Works, founded by Froude over 100 years ago, and the National Maritime Institute at Feltham, had test tanks where we could witness models being towed by gantry, and waves being generated to simulate wind and sea conditions. Water resistance and likely performance of the hull form could then be extrapolated from the model's behaviour for a full-size ship form.

The damage caused by abnormal wave conditions, and specifically freak waves, was highlighted in 1973 by severe structural damage to the Ben Line cargo vessel *Bencruachan* off South Africa, but some of the heaviest losses in high seas have been to bulk carriers. A lengthy enquiry, investigations, underwater examination and model tank tests followed the total loss of the oil and bulk carrier *Derbyshire* in 1980. Bulk carriers, which had typically grown to around 150,000 tonnes deadweight in size, and could have irregular and contrasting weights of cargo loaded in adjoining holds, were

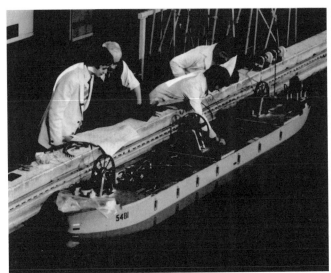

Floating model at the UK's National Maritime Institute used for testing the behaviour of disabled tankers. (*The Naval Architect*, March 1980)

liable to unacceptable longitudinal bending stresses and found to be particularly vulnerable to high seas. The formal investigation into the loss of the *Derbyshire* attributed her foundering to bow flooding and subsequent hatch cover failure. Increased strength requirements for hatch covers and corrugated bulkheads, particularly forward, have since been introduced, and double-skin construction for bulkheads was advocated by several sources including the editorial pages of *The Naval Architect*.

Double-ended roll-on roll-off ships were becoming larger and more versatile in their carriage of lorries, containers and passengers, throughout my years working at RINA, though there were concerns expressed in the journal about the vulnerability of ships with large open car decks to instability if they should become flooded. It was not until years later, in 1987, that the *Herald of Free Enterprise* disaster brought the world's attention to the horrific weakness of 'ro-ro' ferries and prompted RINA to make a public statement drawing attention to their 'unacceptable vulnerability and the likelihood of rapid capsize when car decks are flooded'. The loss of the *Estonia* in a Baltic storm in 1994 caused further shock waves and emphasised the importance of improved bow visor design and watertight bulkheads on car decks.

A revolutionary type of ship launched in the early seventies was the US-designed ocean-going barge carrier, into which ready-loaded barges would be floated for transport across the Atlantic to be floated off at European ports, such as Rotterdam and in the Thames Estuary, for dispersal up river and canal systems. One of these, *Doctor Lykes*, with a length of 874 feet (266m) was, in 1972, the largest American cargo ship ever built.

The new Seabee barge carrier *Doctor Lykes* first sailed from the US Gulf to Europe in 1972. Loaded barges could be floated off from three deck levels. (*The Naval Architect*, October 1972)

On a much smaller scale, manned submersibles for offshore and ocean undersea exploration were also being developed internationally in the early 1970s. And in the field of small craft the Royal National Lifeboat Institution launched, and invited us to see, the new Arun-class self-righting lifeboat. To see a substantial 52-foot craft completely rolled over and right itself was quite a novelty at the time, although self-righting is a standard design feature of modern RNLI lifeboats. Then there were the first rigid inflatable lifeboats: The 21-foot Atlantic 21, which I enjoyed testing out for speed and manoeuvrability in rough weather, was also developed by the RNLI and was the first of an international breed of rigid inflatables which have played a major role in international lifesaving operations and even in policing and fishery interceptions duties ever since.

There was historical interest too in such exploits as the recovery and towing of the hulk of the old Brunel-designed steamship *Great Britain* and her return to Bristol where she is now drydocked as a proud and popular museum ship. Such was the scope of shipbuilding and design which I attempted to record in early issues of *The Naval Architect*.

Another breed of ship which was just coming to the fore was the purpose-built cruise liner which succeeded those passenger ships which, through lack of regular passenger services due to air travel, had been converted for holiday cruising. The 69,529-grt and 316-metre-long *Norway*, which I visited and described in the July 1980 edition of *The Naval Architect*, was at the time the world's largest passenger liner with a capacity for 2,000 passengers. She was in fact the old magnificent transatlantic liner *France* converted at Bremer-

The 69,529grt cruise ship *Norway*, converted from the famous transatlantic liner *France* to accommodate up to 2,000 passengers, the largest passenger ship afloat in 1980. (*The Naval Architect*, July 1980)

haven for Caribbean cruising. Since then new cruise ships have grown steadily in popularity and size with the introduction of luxurious amenities over the ensuing years, to today's undreamt-of sizes, there being no better example than Cunard's 150,000-gt *Queen Mary 2* which entered service in 2004. She is twice the size by volume of the well-known *QE2*. But it hasn't ended there: larger ships such as the *Freedom of the Seas*, with superstructures resembling twelve-storey-high blocks of flats, are even now coming into service.

We included a brief section on warship design within *The Naval Architect* in the early years, for which I recruited the able assistance of Antony Preston, a well-known naval journalist. Our correspondence columns became involved in controversial discussions on the claimed advantages of short, fat rather than long, thin warship hulls, the former advocated by a firm of consultants and much publicised in the popular press, but the traditional Admiralty designs, which RINA supported, won through, as the broader hulls, while providing useful platforms for workboats, would have required unacceptably high gas turbine propulsion power to give satisfactory speeds for such as fast frigates or aircraft carriers.

We also discussed critically, in our naval columns, the design of warships with aluminium superstructures which were more vulnerable to attack by shells or missiles than steel, Aluminium is relatively light above deck and so allows better ship stability with more scope for including upper deck

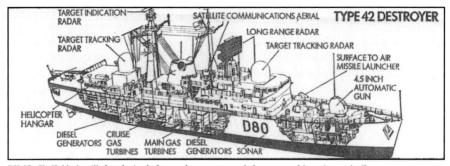

HMS *Sheffield,* the ill-fated air-defence destroyer sunk by a sea-skimming missile.

armament. Our criticism was not entirely appreciated by some shipbuilders, themselves respected members of the Institution, who were at that time building with aluminium as in the superstructures of the Type 21 frigates. There was always a fine line to tread between speaking for the Council of the Institution and adopting press freedom. We could only do what we thought was right and in this case were arguably vindicated by events in the Falklands.

One notable warship in which I went out on trials from Portland into the Channel in 1975 was the ill-fated HMS *Sheffield,* first of the Type 42 guided missile destroyers, and the first RN destroyer propelled by gas turbines. I noted then that she gave an impressive display by accelerating from stopped to a speed of 26 knots in 58 seconds. But in the event she failed in her primary task of providing air defence when in May 1982 she became the first Royal Navy vessel to be sunk in action in almost forty years. Two sea-skimming Exocet missiles from Argentine aircraft penetrated her radar defences. Although on air-defence watch for the British Task Force and equipped with an impressive array of long-range, target-indication and target-tracking radars, she had not detected two launch aircraft, apparently due to a combination of human error and incompatibility between radar and her UHF communications which were then in use, so that only five seconds after the missile target was confirmed an Exocet penetrated above the water-line and set the ship afire with the loss of twenty crew. An official report on the sinking subsequently severely criticised the fire-fighting equipment, training and procedures. A change in RN policy also called for ships that suspected they might be under attack from missiles to turn towards the threat at maximum speed and fire diversionary chaff.

Eventually *Warship Technology* was to be demerged into a separate supplement to the RINA journal so as to give better worldwide coverage of this very exacting science.

Breaking up the daily routine of editorial work on *The Naval Architect* were frequent press conferences on a wide range of maritime events and developments. On one unforgettable occasion in 1978 I went to a buffet lunch in the London Docklands. This was a publicity and fund-raising launch for Ranulph Fiennes' proposed Transglobe Expedition which gave me the opportunity to talk to that intrepid adventurer himself. The aim of the expedition leader was to make a circumpolar journey round the world by sea, land and ice caps via both South and North Poles without flying any part of the way, a feat which had never been attempted before. Fiennes' expedition would follow approximately the axis of the Greenwich Meridian round the Globe making voyages in an ice-strengthened ship between landfalls and ice packs.

To achieve this a great many sponsors were required to provide expeditionary equipment and therefore sales-oriented exhibitions from the ship were arranged to be held at Cape Town, Sydney, Los Angeles and Vancouver during the three-year trip which would also include some scientific survey work. By 1979 some 1,900 sponsors from eighteen countries had rallied round. The insurance brokers C.T. Bowring with strong shipping interests, whose family had sponsored Captain Scott's *Terra Nova* seventy years previously, came to the rescue by buying the thirty-year-old ice-strengthened *Magga Dan* which was renamed *Benjamin Bowring* after an adventurous ancestor of another member of the Bowring family, Anton, who was to recruit the crew. The unpaid crew of merchant seamen were giving up three years of their time to join in this adventure aboard an old, small, slow and uncomfortable ship going to some of the most inhospitable parts of the world. Believe it or not, I did seriously consider joining in with this adventure by offering my services as a watchkeeper but I was told that members of the expedition other than its leader would not be able to write about it for income and instead chose to stick with my job at RINA, where I could follow the expedition's progress with interest from the comfort of my Belgravia desk.

So in September 1979 the *Benjamin Bowring* left Greenwich with its patron, Prince Charles, briefly at the helm. The *New York Times* wrote that the expedition was seven years in the planning and 'leaves England on a journey of such daring that it makes one wonder how the sun ever set on the Empire'. The Transglobe Expedition is described in Fiennes' autobiography, *Mad, Bad and Dangerous*.

Surviving force-8 gales in the Southern Ocean after leaving Cape Town,

Sir Ranulph Fiennes tells me about his projected Transglobe expedition.

the *Benjamin Bowring* duly ploughed into Antarctica in January 1980 where the adventurers were able to step down on to the ice while provisions and their Ski-Doo transports were unloaded. Fiennes' three-man team reached the South Pole in December that year, and the ship again penetrated the ice to pick them up some 2,000 miles away on the far side of Antarctica in January 1981 after they had crossed that Antarctic landmass which is larger than India and China combined. Thence *Benjamin Bowring* sailed to New Zealand and Australia, across the Pacific to Los Angeles and Vancouver, and up to the Bering Strait where, the seas being full of moving ice, the ship had to launch Fiennes' now two-man team with two 12-foot open inflatables at the mouth of the Yukon River. From that river they would navigate the Mackenzie River to its mouth in the Arctic. Then they achieved the incredible feat of making the 3,000-mile route through the fabled North-West Passage up the Canadian archipelago to Ellesmere Island for their ice trek to the North Pole which they finally reached about midnight of 10th April 1982. Thence they went due south to rejoin the *Benjamin Bowring*. The ice-strengthened ship made two attempts to pick them up in the Fram Strait but, in the process, cracked her bow plating in a thick floe. This was cleverly repaired by running the bow up on to the ice to be welded by the ship's engineers. Finally the pickup was made in 80°N on 4th August. From the desolate islands of Spitzbergen it was a straightforward voyage south to the North Sea and the Thames where

Prince Charles again boarded to bring the ship into Greenwich almost exactly three years after her departure.

One unique event I greatly enjoyed in 1979 was a trials flight in a modern airship, the prototype AD-500 from RAF Cardington in Bedfordshire, home of the original British R-100 and R-101 hydrogen-filled airships built between the wars. The helium-filled AD-500 balloon, with a 30ft long (9-m) Kevlar-reinforced gondola below, flanked by two 200-hp Porsche petrol car engines with ducted propellers to give speeds of around 50 knots, had a 2.5-tonne payload. We witnessed air-sea rescue demonstrations from the airship hovering over a reservoir and took a very pleasant flight over the countryside with excellent views from the sloping gondola windows of the ground a few hundred feet below. This airship could have made a good pleasure craft but its main roles were seen as offshore surveillance, anti-smuggling and fishery protection duties, while advertising and photography might have provided further revenue for Airship Industries' craft. But although very economic on fuel there were disadvantages; the payload was modest but most obviously, with so much windage on the balloon, speed and course were very reliant on weather conditions, while mooring to a post at the nose required a lot of space for the airship to swing and could be tricky. Unfortunately Airship Industries, which had been financed by the Australian entrepreneur Alan Bond, was bankrupted and Westinghouse of America took over the technology, eventually building similar Skyships for the US Coast Guard.

We journalists lifted off from Cardington in this prototype airship, 1979.

My years with *The Naval Architect* gave me the opportunity to see a great many new cargo ships, tankers and even large cruise ships, to visit shipyards at home and abroad, and sometimes to go out on trials with new ships. Having, however, stayed with *The Naval Architect* at RINA for just on ten years while bringing out journals with what became monotonous regularity, first quarterly and later bi-monthly, I was getting itchy feet and left to take up freelance writing in July 1980. Working from home, now with a fax machine and the first Amstrad word processor to speed up communications, I enjoyed writing for several different monthly marine technical journals, also for the technical pages of *Lloyd's List*, the world's oldest newspaper, which specialises in shipping news, freight matters and ship movements. I was also able to take a summer off for sailing in the Channel in a fine ketch, an interlude which I recall in the next chapter.

14

Sailing Experiences, Home and Abroad

While working with *The Naval Architect* I spent many weekends sailing, particularly as my services as a navigator were in demand with various yacht owners for sorties around the Solent and cross-Channel trips; I often went out with my old friend Cyril Williams, a dentist and RNR officer. I had originally sailed an Enterprise on Weirwood Reservoir with him, an exercise we pursued even in the depths of winter, which required clearing ice in front of the bow. But then dinghy sailors are a hardy lot.

Later Cyril had this same Enterprise based in Shoreham harbour. One blustery day as we cleared the shelter of the breakwaters and while I was helming and he leaning well out to windward, Cyril was suddenly catapulted, all 13 stone of him, into the sea as the wooden mast snapped bringing down sails and rigging and stopping the boat dead. Cyril clambered back over the transom as the boat started to take on water, and we managed to paddle to the safety of the breakwater.

Eventually Cyril acquired a 22ft MacWester sloop in which, with my sister Rosanna and brother-in law Steve, we sailed out of Littlehampton to Cowes one weekend but on the return leg were caught in a south-westerly gale. We arrived after dark off Littlehampton, but the harbour master warned us off by Morse lamp because there was insufficient water at the river entrance. I was relieved that I had not forgotten my Morse signalling over the years. We hove to for several hours under the storm jib and intermittent engine power until the tide allowed us to approach. Then as we got uncomfortably close to shore to starboard of the entrance channel, we were driven perilously near the roaring breakers close inshore before making the channel. Littlehampton, at the mouth of the river Arun, has a narrow channel with a strong flow which can be up to 6 knots running between the parallel harbour breakwaters and this we had to battle with before we tied up safely in the early hours to break open a bottle of whisky before retiring to our bunks.

The 32ft ketch *White Martlet* in which I made several voyages over the years with Cyril Williams sailing from Chichester across channel and around the Solent and Isle of Wight.

Over the years I was able to enjoy sailing in a series of other boats successively owned by Cyril, including a 27ft MacWester and a 32ft Westerly ketch, *White Martlet,* a very good sea boat he kept at Chichester. Together we went across to Cherbourg and sailed around the Solent. But this waterway became busier and more crowded year by year, as marinas were developed in quieter backwaters such as the Beaulieu River which had been a great favourite of ours particularly on account of its peaceful atmosphere and rich bird life. Finally in 1995 Cyril bought a 32ft Westerly sloop, *Comino 4,* berthed at Birdham, which was very well fitted out with a reliable automatic pilot, Racon radar, and, of course, Sat Nav, the navigational device which was making navigation so easy for the novice. But sailing was still not without its challenges. On one of our most recent expeditions one fine afternoon in August, we set sail for Bembridge in the Isle of Wight, a simple enough crossing from the Chichester basin, fully expecting to be there for supper, but a wall of dense fog suddenly descended as we entered the narrow buoyed channel leading into Bembridge. There were many other boats around starting to sound their sirens and, since we could not even see the next buoy ahead, and to avoid the risk of collision or being stranded on a falling

My wife to be, Patricia, sailing
with friends in the Solent.

tide, we had no choice but to reverse on to a reciprocal course to make the
fairway buoy again. We then inched our way under motor across the main
shipping channel at the eastern approaches to the Solent, sailing between
the No Man's Land and Horse Sand Forts. Still in thick fog, we braved
crossing ferries and other shipping as we headed for Portsmouth which has
the great advantage of offering plenty of water at all tides. Late at night, as
the fog cleared, we docked at the RNSA Marina in Gosport near the naval
training base of HMS *Dolphin*. Instead of a good dinner at Bembridge we
went in search of a late-night Chinese takeaway.

My favourite holidays in the mid-1970s and 80s were, however, spent
flotilla sailing in the Greek islands with a group of friends from London,
my future wife Patricia among them. We sailed around the attractive wooded
Ionian Islands – Corfu, Paxos, Levkas, Kefalonia and Ithaca in particular –
which were at their best in the 1970s before the harbours and inlets became
overcrowded with yachts. One could sail to a bay, deserted or perhaps over-
looked by just one small taverna, there to while away the siesta hour after
swimming, before sailing away in the brisk force 5–6 wind which generally
got up in the afternoon, heading for the next island and supper with a glass
or two of the local ouzo or retsina ashore.

The way in which I originally came to experience flotilla sailing in 1976 was,
to say the least, unusual. I was commuting by moped from Putney along the
King's Road up to town one late summer's day when I saw sailing holidays

advertised in the window of Crawford Perry Travel. Although it was towards the end of the season, I simply went in for a brochure. When they learnt that I had a Master's ticket I was immediately offered a week's free sailing from Corfu with the Flotilla Sailing Club if I would agree to skipper a yacht by day. Five of the staff were going to take one of the 27ft Jaguar boats in the flotilla for the week and I would join them. But one holiday boat had been chartered from the travel agent by a man who worked at the Playboy Club, and was to have skippered a group of four, including two 'bunny girls'. He had, however, been prevented from coming at short notice for some reason I don't recall, and had asked Crawford Perry to find a skipper who would preferably not sleep on that boat. So it was that I had a colourful week sailing with the flotilla but sleeping aboard the travel group's boat. The Crawford Perry party were making arrangements for the following year's brochure and even had a photographer in attendance. They were a very lively bunch and most thought nothing of breakfasting on a pint of Pimm's, which appeared to be the favourite tipple. It was stormy weather, common enough in September, but every morning I would row over to the 'Playboy' yacht, as we sailed in stages around Corfu and Paxos, frequently followed by the photographer in the other boat snapping photographs of our scantily clad passengers for the next year's calendar, in which I appeared in due course, albeit somewhat in the background.

In that short week I became hooked on flotilla sailing. In the ensuing couple of years some of us found it most fun to go in parties of twelve, usually gathered from among friends at the Ski Club of Great Britain, which, directly opposite where I worked at RINA, had become a centre for my social life. Three of us would each skipper a four-berth 27ft Jaguar boat, so that we could explore together and race against each other. Though this was just Mediterranean holiday sailing, with 'navigation for tiny tots', no tides to contend with, no fog and crystal-clear waters, there were frequent occasions when we had to face force 7 winds which could blow up very suddenly. In September, the equinox traditionally brought thunderstorms and torrential rain too, though these storms were generally short-lived.

On one holiday I did get a real shock, for I put a boat aground for the one time in my life. It was a bizarre incident which underlines the rule that one should never take the elements, and particularly the sea, for granted; and also, on a more practical note, that every yacht should be fitted out with some means of measuring the depth of water under the keel, even in the usually clear and tidal free waters of the Mediterranean.

I was with two friends, David and Caroline, in a group flotilla of Jaguar 27s moored in Parga on the west coast of Greece, having sailed across from the island of Paxos. We had a free afternoon and, it being a fine sunny day with just a light onshore breeze, we were recommended to visit a sheltered shallow bay a few miles east in which we were told by the local flotilla leader we could anchor safely. Unfortunately none of the other boats chose to accompany us, as we could have easily helped one another. The Admiralty chart showed one fathom of water close to the shore in the bay and our draft was about 4 feet, so there should have been sufficient water in the approaches to the bay. The river Styx, no less, ran into this sandy bay, providing fresh water, which greatly appealed to Caroline who wanted an opportunity to wash her hair. But, unusually for that coast, the water was not clear and we had no echo sounder so, having downed sail about a hundred yards from shore, I was about to turn under motor to drop anchor when we felt the boat's keel touch bottom. Engine full astern surprisingly did not free us as we had apparently run into a soft sandbank. Neither did it help putting 6ft 4in tall David overside to lighten load and give us a push, for just then the wind got up, tending to drive us closer inshore, while uncannily also at that moment the clouds gathered, short angry waves formed and

I meet up with my parents for a sail at Corfu on a flotilla holiday.

the elements seemed eerily to conspire, sensing their moment to claim a victim. Wading through the water, I carried out a kedge anchor astern and we tried to use this to haul us off, all to no avail.

We tried everything but the wind, now a fresh force 5 would immediately drive us aground again after the slightest hint of floating; so David waded ashore and went off to get assistance from the locals, which was not forthcoming. From thence he went by taxi from the nearest village back to Parga to get another of our boats to pull us off. However, it was getting late when the flotilla leader, Martin Evans, motored into the bay and, after trying unsuccessfully to tow us out stern first, put a line round our mast to heel our boat over thus tilting the keel off the sandbank. But under these conditions the tactic proved disastrous as, despite the other boat trying to pull us clear, we were instantly driven even closer inshore by wind and sea, and, now with the hull listed towards the weather, water broke over our decks and into the cabin. Evening came, so while the leader's boat returned to Parga, there to order a tug for the next day, the three of us were forced to abandon ship with whatever dry goods we could and make camp on the beach for the night; there we could at least keep an eye on our boat and protect it from the predatory natives who had done nothing to help us.

Although on this occasion I had been responsible for just a small leisure boat, I felt, during that long cold and miserable night, something of the despair that every skipper or captain who has ever lost his ship must feel. And, thereafter when sailing a charter boat I always made myself a lead line – standard equipment on any ship – from a weighted cord marked along its length with bunting so that I could measure water depth whenever in doubt.

When I left *The Naval Architect* in 1980 to work freelance I was, after ten years, free from the shackles of printers' deadlines and journal production. I decided to take advantage of this and, as summer approached in 1981, treated myself to a summer job as skipper/caretaker of a beautiful 51ft McGruer ketch, *Border Legend*, for a season. I say 'beautiful' with good reason because she was a traditional wooden-built yacht with fine lines; her hull was varnished from stem to stern; she had teak decks, and varnished mahogany upperworks. Maintaining the hull in good condition was always going to be a challenge but it was worth it for the admiring looks we attracted at each anchorage or harbour we visited.

The owner worked for Guinness Peat in London and wanted to sail the boat with friends and family throughout spare time and holidays in the summer. *Border Legend* was based in Camper & Nicholsons' yard at Gosport from where she would be able to sail freely out into the Solent or cross-

Channel without being restrained by tidal restrictions.

We had our share of adventures during that summer. One Friday evening the owner with six male colleagues from his firm came aboard in Gosport complete with their dinner suits, intent on attending a business dinner in Paris that Saturday night. The wind was right on the nose as we headed out of the Solent for our planned crossing to Cherbourg so we had to divert eastwards to Deauville, which at least allowed us to get a good sail on the starboard tack. We made port safely on Saturday morning; the party put on their glad rags and took a train to Paris while I stocked up with duty-frees from the local supermarket and stowed the bottles in the bilges – ship's supplies for the summer ahead. Having successfully completed their mission, our party rejoined *Border Legend* on Sunday and we set off in the afternoon so that they would be able to catch an early train the next day from Portsmouth to London. The night was calm, so we motored but soon ran into thick fog, and I was up all night watching the radar screen, listening for fog sirens and looking out for any lights as we crossed the busy shipping lanes in the Channel.

Not many sailing yachts were equipped with radar in 1981 and we were lucky to have even a simple set, although a look at the screen with its dozens of pinpoint echoes all around from ships crossing both ways, as well as fishing vessels and other yachts and small craft, all within our 12-mile range of radar vision, is really alarming as many overnight cross-channel sailors will know. Surprisingly we managed to keep to our schedule and my crew of passengers all got to work on Monday morning, no doubt having taken for granted the successful outcome of this rather risky timetable.

Although not seriously prepared for it, we also took part at the owner's whim in June that summer in the Round-the-Island race, that jamboree in which each year yachts of all shapes and sizes make an anticlockwise circuit of the Isle of Wight. I readied the boat at short notice on Friday and when our party arrived we sailed out to an anchorage in the Solent, keen and ready for the morning start. There was a brisk wind from the east and the dozens of boats running under their colourful spinnakers were a breathtaking sight in the morning sunlight. The fun really started when we got down to the Needles, that line of tall rocks extending from the white cliffs to a lighthouse at the south-western tip of the island. As the boats turned sharply to port as close to the Needles as they dared, they had to adjust to the changing wind direction by taking in their spinnakers to sail under main and jib. Our owner had just acquired a new spinnaker but had not until this time had a chance to use it; so with our scratch crew we were, not surprisingly, among the many boats that fouled their spinnakers on the rigging and lost valuable time; we had never been in serious contention anyway and when the wind eased to force 3 our large wooden seven-berth cruising boat was far too heavy to make good way in such a gentle breeze. Furthermore, everyone was required to take his turn at the wheel and some were less conscientious than others. There was a small black-and-white portable television set on board and one helmsman actually set it up to watch Wimbledon tennis as we made a lazy afternoon leg from St Catherine's back towards the finishing line.

The boss then decided he wanted to make his way down the French coast to the Channel Islands and Brittany. This involved initially a weekend crossing to Fécamp, where he and his companions left me for a week, moored alongside a pontoon in the harbour. There are some places one takes an instant liking to, and Fécamp was one of those. The harbour master's daughter, no doubt attracted by our handsome boat, came aboard and offered to show me round. There were the Benedictine distillery in the town and some interesting cliff walks with concrete German coastal gun emplacements still very much in evidence. I acquired a few provisions and the following weekend back came the owner, this time with his wife and daughter, and we set off down Channel, now with fresh to strong easterly winds to push us along.

Running before the wind we made a quick passage to the Seine estuary, where I incurred the only slight injury in all my years of seagoing. We decided to put into Honfleur on a wet and windy morning; I spotted the fairway buoy with my binoculars and gave orders to turn to port to enter the Seine River; then with the boss on the wheel, I stepped down from the cockpit to check the chart. The boat pitched heavily in the rough waters as the wind and seas came round to our bow. As I climbed back up from the cabin to cockpit, binoculars around my neck, I caught one foot on the stormboard, my knee came up and pushed the binoculars – actually a long pair of Rommel's powerful desert army glasses acquired in the Lanes of Brighton some years before – straight into my mouth, breaking my two front teeth. This rather spoilt our stay in Honfleur for me, a pity as it is a most popular little haven for yachtsmen with an attractive medieval town, in total contrast to the industrial chimneys of Le Havre passed on the way upriver.

After some forty-eight hours with more pleasant weather we resumed our sail westwards, calling at Cherbourg where the family left to go home. Then the boss and I carried on alone to Alderney, where we anchored among many other yachts in the Great Harbour with its long northern breakwater. The wind was blowing a strong north-easterly by now and that was, unfortunately, the one direction from which the anchorage is unprotected. I ferried the boss ashore in our inflatable to catch a plane home, though I'm afraid he got a bit wet in the process. Then I was left alone with the boat for a week. There was a bit of maintenance to do and provisions to acquire, but I was obviously not going to have a very sociable time as, in that unsettled weather, it was impossible to take the dinghy without getting very wet. However, there was a harbour boat service and I was able to get to a dentist, a very sympathetic lady, who fixed me up with caps on my front teeth as good as new, this without charging me a penny.

The one big event of my stay in Alderney was the Royal Wedding of Charles and Diana in 1981. The residents of that island don't need much excuse for drinking but this really was a late night. As, that day, the wind and rain lashed the boat and the dinghy was half full of water I stayed alone onboard and I put out a second anchor for safety, then settled down over a glass of wine and tin of minced beef to watch the procession and later the fireworks in Hyde Park, perhaps not seen to their best in black and white on a 7-inch screen with poor reception; it all seemed a million miles away.

Boats all around had made a great effort to dress ship with bunting streaming from all their halyards and between masts, and a very cheerful sight it made during that afternoon of the wedding. I was more restrained about putting up flags as the weather forecast was still bad, and sure enough the wind blew up into a storm during the night. There was plenty of activity as tenders returned to their boats during the small hours. Yachts were yawing frantically to their anchors and I went on deck at daybreak next morning to see, close by, a very worried gentleman in his pyjamas staring alternately between his heaving anchor chain and the tangle of flags hanging from his masts, which were quite obviously beyond retrieving. There were a great many sore heads early that morning as Alderney recovered from its collective hangover.

At the end of the week the boss flew back to the boat to sail with me to Guernsey and, now with the prevailing westerly winds, we headed for St Peter Port. However, he had a tight schedule; indeed I admired his perseverance in making these weekend forays at all. So that he could fly home on Sunday afternoon we anchored off the north tip of the island and I took him ashore in the dinghy. This left me to arrange a berth in the new small marina near La Fontenelle, and to borrow two lads from ashore to handle our mooring lines. The entrance to this marina is a narrow passage, not more than the length of our own boat in width, which opens out into a bowl blasted out of the rock. To motor in through the narrow entrance between high rock walls without being able to see right through, while sounding the ship's horn, and at sufficient speed to control steerage despite the following swell and tidal drift, was one of the more hazardous manoeuvres I had to make with a boat of that size. In fact, she glided in beautifully. As the marina opened out I put the helm hard over to port, engine in neutral gear and she drifted neatly alongside the nearest pontoon without, to my relief, any blemish to her varnished hull.

I remained there until the next weekend, taking the local buses to see a bit of the island. Then the owner's family boarded, mother, daughter and son, and we sailed down the coast to St Peter Port. The weather had finally cleared up and the family had a chance for a real summer holiday at last. This took in a cruise to Jersey and Sark, where we anchored in a beautiful bay and were able to walk around that peaceful traffic-free island. Then on to St-Malo with its old fortress walls and into the river Rince through the tidal barrier with its high-rising lock before sailing back from St-Malo to the Hamble, where I left *Border Legend* in the hands of her now-experienced owner. That was really my last major sailing experience apart from the occasional few days' holidays in home waters in later years.

15

To Work in the Netherlands and Back

Following that summer of sailing in 1981, I went back to freelance writing but was soon, rather unfortunately, persuaded to take on the creation of another journal to be named *Combat Craft*. This would cover technical developments in all the small craft involved in military, policing and offshore patrol duties, an interesting enough subject which brought me into closer contact with the world of naval and military events. The journal was to be published alongside a more established journal, *Hovering Craft and Hydrofoil*, which our new publisher had just taken over.

We had a grand start with offices in Garrick Street by Covent Garden in one of the liveliest parts of London. I was able to visit warships, defence establishments and naval exhibitions around the world. So far so good, but I had no regular staff to assist me in the production of this bi-monthly journal and our inexperienced publisher was soon overstretching himself, being unable to get the support of advertisers, while our specialised field only commanded an initial circulation of some 3,000 copies. The London office was abandoned after a few months and I was asked to produce the editorial from my home flat in Putney, which I did for a while. But after two years, when the publisher found he could no longer pay me, I resisted the offer to take on publication of the journal myself, with all the financial implications involved. Instead *Combat Craft* was absorbed as a small craft section into *Navy International*, a prestigious enough monthly technical journal for which I continued to write. But economic conditions and competition were tough for all small privately run publishing houses; both *Navy International* and its traditional rival, *Maritime Defence*, for which I had also written from time to time, were soon to fold under competition from the rapidly expanding Jane's Information Group, best known for its annual *Jane's Fighting Ships*, but now producing annual, monthly and even weekly defence books and magazines.

I now enjoyed a period of more carefree writing, albeit of irregular income, for both US and British journals including some freelance articles for the RINA. Then in 1986 I was tempted by an advertisement for a Scientific Editor required at an attractive tax-free salary by NATO's SHAPE (Supreme Headquarters, Allied Powers Europe) Technical Center (STC) in The Hague. So I went over there for an interview and was offered the position.

There followed a prolonged period of, in my view, rather ridiculous security vetting, during which my closest friends were asked all sorts of personal questions about me and therefore thought I was about to become a most important secret agent. Having survived this scrutiny, I let my flat in January 1987 and went across to The Hague, taking lodgings at Scheveningen, the seaside residential suburb of The Hague. To my dismay I found this new 9–5 job stultifyingly bureaucratic. I was deskbound, unable to get about as I had hoped, being merely required to turn into more fluent English those classified technical papers, written by scientists politically selected from all the different NATO nations during those dying years of the Cold War.

It was, however, a comfortable enough existence. The Hague was not very inviting in that first long grey winter, the ground continuously frozen brown but, when summer came, well-tended parks blossomed, and the tulip fields sparkled with colour. The transport system was excellent; I cycled a lot and the network of trams stretched as far as the picturesque town of Delft. There were art galleries and museums, particularly my favourite Mauritshaus, home of Vermeer's *Girl with a Pearl Earring*, close by the Parliament buildings. There were well-ordered flower gardens, which only the Dutch can keep so tidily, and long walks along the beach, with opportunities for plenty of swimming at weekends and after work – albeit in somewhat murky brown North Sea water; after all we were only 15 miles from Rotterdam, Europe's biggest port. I was also to enjoy the many delightful beachside pancake houses which sprang up for about 2 miles along the seafront at Scheveningen in the summer, only to be dismantled in the autumn. Then there was no end of places to eat in the evenings particularly if one enjoyed Indonesian food.

While I was living and working in The Hague I had the opportunity to take up art classes seriously, and painting has been one of my favourite pastimes ever since. I joined a small mixed group of Dutch, British and other nationalities, taking evening classes in oil painting, very often with a model to work from in portrait or life drawing. Our art teacher, Annilees, was a charming and very talented Dutch lady artist and half a dozen of us really looked forward to our evenings in her attic art studio which always managed to exude a romantic impressionist atmosphere. As a result of these sessions I even produced, for the first time, a few paintings that I was able to sell, mostly of the bulb fields and nearby woods.

Although visited by my friends and family whom one enjoyed showing round, I was nonetheless homesick, and frequently flew back to London for weekends, renewing my acquaintance with Patricia, my good friend and neighbour from Putney days. Coming home for a long Easter break the following year I proposed and we married that July, honeymooning in *Sound of Music* country in the Austrian Alps. Patricia then came over to live in The Hague where she joined the circle of ex-pat wives from Britain and America.

We played a good deal of tennis with the Commonwealth Club, swam a lot from the long sandy beach in the summer months, and visited many of the towns around the Netherlands. It was a good life but never likely to be permanent while our roots and relatives were in England. There was also the problem of our two Putney flats, which were only let on a temporary basis.

So in the summer of 1990 Patricia and I returned to London to make our home in Putney. Back there I resumed my maritime journalistic work, taking on among other jobs, the editorship of *Warship Technology* for the RINA, the latter a more recent offshoot of *The Naval Architect*. This naval journal covers the design and outfitting of all types of military ships, from aircraft carriers to the smallest craft for anti-smuggling duties, fast missile attack craft, frigates and diesel or nuclear-powered submarines capable of spending long periods underwater. Inevitably there became progressively more coverage of electronics as traditional ship's navigation bridges, operational control rooms and weapons systems were transformed into batteries of computer monitors.

One notable innovation which made economic sense was combining the work and techniques of merchant and naval shipbuilding yards to build the helicopter carrier, HMS *Ocean,* which could be used for military or disaster relief duties by the Royal Navy and is in service today. Kvaerner on the Clyde built the hull which was then towed to Barrow-in-Furness for naval outfitting out by Vickers' shipyard.

Replacements for the Royal Navy's three refurbished Invincible-class carriers were already under discussion while I was Editor and there were several competing artists' impressions of the Navy's future aircraft carriers – although these ships are still at the planning stage more than fifteen years later and the debate on affordability continues unabated. However, with the most recently announced Government intent to go ahead, design proposals have at last hardened to two 65,000-ton carriers with 920ft long flight decks.

At Brest I got to visit the mammoth nuclear-powered aircraft carrier *Charles de Gaulle,* pride of the French fleet, and, by contrast, had a lively day out from Lorient in new offshore patrol vessels built for Morocco. The latter

Combining merchant and naval shipbuilding techniques, the Royal Navy's helicopter carrier *Ocean* launched by Kvaerner on the Clyde in 1995 for fitting out by Vickers at Barrow. (*Photo* VSEL)

adopted the latest innovation of launching and recovering fast rigid inflatable interception boats from a stern ramp, a system which added greatly to the operational effectiveness of patrol vessels involved in fishery protection and combating drug smuggling.

There was by now a strong emphasis on stealth in ship design to protect against radar detection, with hull plates angled away from the vertical, clean contours and unencumbered superstructures. In larger warships spaces were included for protection against nuclear blast and outer surfaces could be washed down to counteract radiation.

Other innovations of the 1990s, yet to come to full potential, were the designs of catamaran and even trimaran hull types, already common enough in small craft, but now intended for larger oceangoing ships. We have of course since become familiar with fast catamaran ferries, although these are

A La Fayette class French escort frigate designed for stealth with superstructure inclined at 10 deg. to the vertical to reduce radar echoes, 1995.

not proving to be so reliable in rough weather. Further developments of the 1990s were in the small waterplane area twin-hull (SWATH) ship built for speed by the US Navy and the heavy-duty semi-submerged twin-hull type of ship, which has its main buoyancy chambers or bulbs at a depth just below the waves and therefore provides a stable platform, very useful for offshore work.

In 1992, thanks to improved communications through the fax machine, which enabled me to work from home, Patricia and I were able to sell up our individual Putney flats and move to the delightful rural village of Alfriston in the heart of the South Downs, with its welcome rolling countryside and sea air. I was able to keep my freelance writing and editing going for a few years, thanks to new computer developments and the village post office, through which I was, surprisingly, generally able to keep to an overnight service with printers and publishers.

Alfriston is close to our mutual roots in Sussex, just a few miles from where Patricia had been brought up in Bexhill and my own childhood home in Rushlake Green, which has changed little since. The Cuckmere Valley, designated an Area of Outstanding Natural Beauty, and now an integral part of a new National Park, stretches down to the sea which is about 5 miles away. The meandering tidal river varies between a few feet and several fields in width when flooded, and the sea can be seen from the top of our hill on the South Downs Way.

16

Reflections upon the Sea, Sailors and Ships

A wanderer is man from his birth,
He was born in a ship
On the breast of the river of Time.

The Future, Matthew Arnold

My early days at sea were not the happiest; there were long hours, days, even weeks, of boredom, particularly on tankers which spent so little time in port, but I learned a lot from that period of my life. Reading – we had to thank the Seafarers Education Service for providing a library on board – was one of the few recreations. And yet we crew got so used to our small world within the confines of the ship that we almost resented the hubbub and intrusion of people rushing aboard when we arrived in port. Seafarers were always restless to be at sea when stuck in port, yet keen to get home when too long at sea.

Sailors tended to be philosophical; they had time to think and were drawn close to nature, particularly on those long night hours when on watch under the stars. We were deeply aware too of the nature of the sea varying in mood between smooth and calm, friendly, bright and breezy, eerie, aggressive and even violent; colours constantly changing from the magic of early dawn through grey and golden, transparent green and blues. The weather, throwing wind, spray and sometimes green seas at us, dominated our lives. And in my subsequent boat-sailing experiences I could recognise the addiction that the sea has for lone and long distance sailors.

Some sailed over the ocean in ships,
earning their living on the seas.
They saw what the Lord can do,
his wonderful acts on the seas.

Psalm 107

When I joined Royal Mail, life became more colourful and enjoyable, the ships were busier, morale was high, the West Indian and South American ports had an exotic appeal and we reflected the excitement that our passengers felt. I was very sorry to leave the South American cargo-passenger service as that era drew to its close. I have written for the most part about the two shipping companies with which I sailed but going back fifty and more years there were dozens of different independent companies within the British Merchant Navy alone, each boasting their own house flags, colours and distinctive funnel markings, and a great variety of ships designed to carry general cargo around the world. Ocean-going passenger ships employed beauty and style in their hull lines, decor and general appearance as well as speed, to attract custom as they competed in the serious business of transporting people between continents.

The officers and crews who made life-time careers of serving in the fleets of prestigious liner companies kept up their own proud traditions. Their ships, and those of more humble shipping lines too, were manned by seamen who served so resolutely during the two world wars while thousands, unsung heroes, lost their lives at sea. Individual ships had remarkable war records not only in the crucial task of bringing food and supplies to our island but also as troop transports and hospital ships. In the following appendices I refer to those activities within the Stanhope Steamship and Royal Mail fleets, but there were many more heroics throughout the Merchant Navy which could fill volumes.

No wonder nostalgia is strong among ex-seafarers and lovers of ships. This was brought home to me most vividly when Patricia and I recently went on an unforgettable voyage aboard MV *Discovery*, sailing from Manaus, 1,000 miles up the steamy Amazon via Devils Island and the West Indies to the UK, with a party of 200 ex-seafarers and their families including several retired ship captains in a group organised by Maritime Memories. All with a common interest in the sea, we were treated to a feast of lectures and recollections while aboard this traditional passenger ship.

When I came to make my living ashore I was lucky to find myself working side-by-side with men who had been at sea and to become involved with the naval architects and marine engineers responsible for the design and construction of ships. One can only admire their quest to improve ships and the safety of life at sea.

Ship design has changed dramatically over the past sixty years and for obvious reasons. The explosion in building standard utility ships as quickly as possible during the war years, particularly in the United States, has led to a more economic approach to design. Ship construction has become more basic – to put it very simply a flat hull plate is easier to make and install than a precisely curved one. Economy of scale has led to much larger ships, particularly among tankers as world trade has increased; the container revolution has completely changed the design and operation of cargo ships and their terminal ports; the carriage of mail by sea, which led to the very creation of Royal Mail, has evaporated, and the traditional passenger ship has given way to high-tiered cruise ships where the emphasis is on carrying vast numbers and providing as much on-board entertainment as possible rather than enjoying the ship for its own sake.

Though less outwardly visible, a new sophistication and vast technical improvements have, of course, since evolved in safety measures, ship control systems, satellite navigational equipment and worldwide communications. It is difficult now to believe that we relied so heavily on the sun and the stars for our ocean crossings. In conclusion I can only thank my stars for having had such an interesting life.

Appendix 1

Highlights in the History of the
Stanhope Steamship Company

Jack Billmeir's Stanhope Steamship Company was a very opportunistic tramping firm which had been founded in 1934 with the purchase of two old cargo ships of around 700 tons each, namely the SS *Sandhill* and SS *Wooler*. Thereafter the company had made big money by running Franco's blockade during the Spanish Civil War and there were even some shipmasters in the company, such as the notorious 'Potato Jones', who were reported to have concealed arms in their cargoes of foodstuffs for Spain.

By 1938 the number of ship's under Stanhope's blue-and-white 'JAB' house flag, which sported a blue B on a white band across the black funnel, had grown to eighteen. During the ensuing Second World War, Stanhope lost twenty of its own ships and another twelve Government ships manned and managed by the company, mostly torpedoed, mined or attacked by aircraft, with the loss of 233 lives altogether.

A typical wartime replacement 1943, the motor ship *Stanpark*.

The ship casualties were, however, replaced during and after the war with new tonnage. Among them were the *Stanfirth*, formerly an Admiralty aircraft engine repair ship, and the *Stanroyal*, formerly a 12,300-tons deadweight German merchant vessel *Isar*, built in Hamburg in 1929, which had been a PoW transport during the war, then commandeered in reparation. While the *Stanroyal* was being converted at the Tyneside yard of Palmers Hebburn Co. Ltd, a scribbled note was found on a storeroom bulkhead indicating that '14 men, 5 NCOs and one officer of the Second Battalion Queens Royal Regiment' were imprisoned there in July 1942. Post-war the converted and refurbished *Stanfirth* and *Stanroyal* now boasted limited passenger accommodation, a step up the ladder socially for this tramp company.

So, by 1948, during the first post-war shipping boom, Billmeir was well placed with a relatively modern fleet of nineteen modern cargo vessels and tankers. These included several cargo ships acquired during the war years and since converted from coal burners to oil fuel, as well as four tankers. These ships were chartered out worldwide, some by the voyage, some on time charter. This was the fleet as it stood when I joined the company.

Company records show that in the year of 1948 the fleet steamed 733,893 miles and carried 878,819 tons of cargo, of which 270,688 tons were liquids (mainly crude fuel and diesel oil), 208,878 tons were coal and 206,905 tons were cereals (mainly grain from Australia and Canada). There were also 85,607 tons of ores and phosphates, 56,448 tons of timber, and 38,000 tons of general cargo comprising mainly manufactured and consumer goods. Then by 1952 the fleet was joined by two newly built cargo ships from Burntisland, Sunderland, *Stanhope* and *Stanburn*, in both of which I was later to serve as a cadet.

The heroic wartime endeavours of the crews of Stanhope's ships, against overwhelming odds, mirror the wider and hardly appreciated contribution of all merchant seamen who served under the Red Ensign during the war. These events were recorded in a company brochure produced in 1948 that I was given upon joining the company.

Stanhope's first casualty occurred very early in the war; on 19th November 1939 the 2,600-ton *Stanbrook* was mined when sailing between Antwerp and the Tyne with the loss of all hands. During the war years Stanhope ships provided early shipping aid to France and Belgium, participated in the perilous Narvik trade, sailed to Singapore and Batavia, and took their place in convoys and on lone voyages with volunteer crews to the relief of Malta. They were involved in the Battle of the Atlantic and made unescorted winter passages to Archangel and Murmansk; they supplied the fighting forces in India and the Mediterranean, and carried some of the first troops and equipment to the Normandy beaches. Many of Stanhope's officers and crew were decorated including two captains who received the DSO. Many other of the company's captains, officers and crew received DSC, DSM, OBE, MBE, BEM decorations or Mention in Dispatches.

Typical of the heroic exploits of these merchantmen was Stanhope's *Parracombe*, which attempted the first unescorted passage to Malta with a cargo of Government stores but was, according to Stanhope's own records, attacked by forty Heinkel aircraft. Thirty of the forty-seven crew were lost. Another recent book on the Malta convoys claims that, flying a Spanish flag, then a French flag when off the coast of Tunisia, the *Parracombe* was in fact carrying twenty crated Beaufighters and ammunition. According to this report she was struck by mines, eighteen survivors being picked up, some by a Fleet Air Arm flying boat, others by the Vichy French in Tunisia. Two other ships managed by the company, *Empire Defender* and *Empire Pelican*, were both lost in attempts to reach Malta early in 1941.

Another Company-managed ship, *Empire Guillemot*, had the distinction of being the first merchant ship actually to succeed in reaching Malta unescorted. She docked there with relief supplies in September 1941, after employing various ruses to counter the unwelcome attention of enemy planes and ships. The Governor of the island, Sir William Dobbie, thanked the Master and crew personally on arrival. But, two days after leaving Malta she was machine-gunned and bombed by three Italian planes. A bomb went clean through No.5 hatch and she began to sink immediately. The Captain and crew took to the boats, hoping to make it to Gibraltar about 600 miles away, but were forced to land in Algeria where they were interned until liberated by the Allied armies two years later.

The Admiralty soon realised that the dice were too heavily loaded against making successful unescorted voyages to Malta. In fact, my uncle James Burnett sailed as a naval liaison officer aboard a Stanhope-managed cargo ship in November 1941; this was the third of four ships being sent separately to Malta with supplies at weekly intervals. His duty was to decode messages from the Admiralty, see that camouflage procedures were implemented – this was intended to include painting a series of false nations' flags on the hulls when in the Mediterranean – and take responsibility for the gun defence system. Only the naval officer could give orders to open fire using the sole armament on board, in this case just twin Oerlikons on each bridge wing. However, when news was received that the first two of the four ships had both been sunk by the enemy between Gibraltar and

Malta, the plan was thankfully abandoned and my uncle was able to return to regular naval duties in the Western Approaches. Decorated with DSC and Bar, he survived the war.

The plight of Malta in 1941–42 became desperate with ships unable to reach the island fortress unescorted and with heavy losses when in convoy. A particularly strenuous but disastrous effort was made in August 1942 when a convoy left Gibraltar with fourteen merchant ships and an escort at various times of two battleships, three aircraft carriers, six cruisers, and no fewer than fourteen destroyers. The carrier *Eagle* was the first to be sunk, by a U-boat, then nine merchant ships, two cruisers and a destroyer were also lost.

A fine example of the tenacity shown by the Stanhope crews was made apparent when a small cargo ship, *Stanlake*, was torpedoed by E-boats 5 miles south of the Lizard in April 1943. The crew were picked up by a minesweeper and landed at Falmouth Bay. Yet, within forty-eight hours the Master and several crew were back at sea in another of the Stanhope vessels, *Stanforth*. This was typical of the courageous attitude of the British merchant seamen throughout the war.

Elsewhere, the 9,200-ton *Stanpark* was overtaken and captured by the German battleship *Admiral Scheer*, which then sank the ship by gunfire. The crewmen were transferred to the German prison ship *Porland* which they, with the other prisoners, made a gallant attempt to seize. When this failed they attempted to set fire to the *Porland*, but the men were overpowered, tied to stanchions in the hold and flogged. Two prisoners were murdered and three later sentenced by the Germans to terms of imprisonment of up to twenty years.

Among other casualties, the 2,350-ton *Stanmore* was torpedoed by a German submarine while on passage to Italy in October 1943. Temporarily abandoned, she was later found to be still afloat but sinking. She was towed to North Africa, beached and the entire cargo salved.

A sistership, *Stanwell*, almost survived the war. After making many hazardous journeys across the Atlantic, she was sent with a cargo of Government stores to Port Tewfik in 1942 at the time Rommel was threatening Alexandria. Mines exploded around her and she was badly damaged but the crew managed to get the *Stanwell* out of port and bring her home. Her end was inglorious but useful; she was sunk as a blockship off the Normandy beaches in 1944. Meanwhile one of the first ships to proceed to the Normandy beach head to be used as a blockship was the Stanhope-managed *Empire Tamar*. Heavily involved in the D-Day action was the Stanhope-managed *Empire Lough*, which was attacked and set on fire off Dover when taking her third cargo of high explosives to the Normandy beaches. Captain Robinson MBE remained on board until his crew were safely in the boats, then jumped into the blazing sea but died soon after being picked up.

Two American-built tankers of 16,584 deadweight, the *Fort Cheswell* and *Fort Jupiter*, both 'T2' turbo-electric tankers (TET) built by the Sun Shipbuilding Co. in 1945, were acquired by the company from the US Maritime Commission in 1947. In honour of their wartime predecessors, they were named *Stanwell* and *Stanmore* respectively and it was to this TET *Stanwell* that I was first appointed.

The T2 fleet of standard design tankers, some 536 in number, had been mass-produced in various US shipyards to carry oil to Europe for the Allies in the latter half of the war as part of the Maritime Commission's emergency programme; they had turbo-electric propulsion because this gave a good speed of up to 15 knots but at the same time obviated the need for the more complicated construction of mechanical reduction gearing.

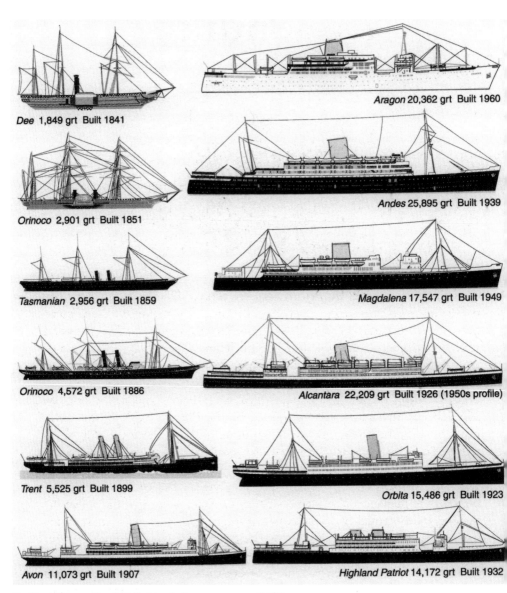

Dee 1,849 grt Built 1841

Orinoco 2,901 grt Built 1851

Tasmanian 2,956 grt Built 1859

Orinoco 4,572 grt Built 1886

Trent 5,525 grt Built 1899

Avon 11,073 grt Built 1907

Aragon 20,362 grt Built 1960

Andes 25,895 grt Built 1939

Magdalena 17,547 grt Built 1949

Alcantara 22,209 grt Built 1926 (1950s profile)

Orbita 15,486 grt Built 1923

Highland Patriot 14,172 grt Built 1932

Profiles of some Royal Mail ships built over a span of 120 years.

Appendix 2

The Origins and History of Royal Mail Lines

Royal Mail's seagoing services extended for more than 120 years from 1840 onwards. Over this time the company's ships evolved from pioneering wooden paddle-steamers to screw-propelled and motor cargo ships and fast liners, between them carrying mails, passengers, troops, bullion and general and refrigerated cargoes all over the world. They also provided exceptional contributions to their country in the Crimea, Boer War and two world wars, several of the larger ships having been requisitioned as armed merchant cruisers, troop carriers or hospital ships. Eventually, however, in the late 1960s Royal Mail Lines was taken over by the Furness Withy Group and, not long after, by a Hong Kong consortium. So the company and its ships ultimately faded away around 1970, alas along with the bulk of merchant shipping under the Red Ensign.

Royal Mail was conceived by James MacQueen, from Lanarkshire, who became the manager of a sugar estate in Grenada where, in the 1820s, he realised the potential of steamships for inter-island communication in the Caribbean. Returning to Glasgow in 1830 and frustrated by the slow and unreliable service provided by Admiralty sailing brigs for carrying mail, he campaigned for a line of Royal Mail steamers. In 1838 MacQueen approached the Treasury with proposals for establishing Royal Mail steamer services to the West Indies and the following year, with financial backing from the Government-sponsored West Indies Committee, the first meeting of the Royal Mail Steam Packet Company (RMSP) was held at the premises of merchant bankers Reid, Irving & Co. in London; John Irving MP subsequently became RMSP's first Chairman.

On 26th September 1839 Queen Victoria granted a Royal Charter incorporating the company. The Royal Coat of Arms thereafter formed a part of the company's livery and its distinctive house flag came to include a Royal crown in the centre of a red St Andrew's cross on a white background. The new house flag was to be first flown at the launch of the RMSP's vessel *Leith* in May 1841.

The development of steamships designed to carry out regular mail services was not without its hazards and disasters. A major stumbling block in the early days was the Admiralty's specification of wooden hulls, although RMSP had indicated its own preference for building iron hulls.

A contract was duly signed by the Admiralty in 1840 for a twice-monthly steamship service to Barbados, Grenada, Santa Cruz, St Thomas, Nicole Mole, Santiago de Cuba and Port Royal in Jamaica; the latter port was later renamed Kingston and would remain Royal Mail's principal West Indian port for the next 120 years.

The original contract, involving annual steaming of more than 684,000 miles, required the provision of fourteen steamships and three sailing ships plus bunkering and repair facilities. It also called for the first mail sailing by 1st December 1841. A single design was selected for the initial fleet of fourteen wooden hulled paddle-steamers, which were built at yards in Greenock, Northfleet, Bristol, Leith and Cowes. The hulls were constructed of British and African oak with iron fastenings and were copper-sheathed against Toredo worm. At approximately 1,850 gross tons each, these vessels were somewhat larger than the 1,340-gt *Great Western,* Isambard Kingdom Brunel's famous pioneering transatlantic paddle-steamer.

Having been built at Bristol in 1837, four years earlier, for the Great Western Steamship Co., the *Great Western* was a 236ft long four-masted paddle-steamer with accommodation for up to 148 passengers and was already making history with regular voyages to New York, her Atlantic crossings averaging about fifteen days.

The first ships of the Royal Mail fleet measured 275 feet (83.82 metres) overall from bowsprit to taffrail and 60 feet (18.29 metres) in width over the paddle boxes. Propulsion power was provided by 2-cylinder 400-hp engines supplied with steam by four boilers giving ship speeds of up to 9 knots. In these pioneering days of steam propulsion, the ships still carried a three-masted barquentine sailing rig, the foremast alone being square rigged, although later most were converted to brigs, with square-rigged fore and main masts. Up to a hundred passengers could be carried.

The first company steamer *Clyde*, the largest ship built on the Clyde to that time, sailed from Southampton to the West Indies on 18th December 1841, and the *Thames* carried the first mails from Falmouth on 3rd January 1842 for Berbice, Havana, New York and Halifax. Thereafter mail steamers left twice monthly for Atlantic crossings averaging nineteen days with coaling stops at Corunna and Madeira outward and Bermuda homeward. New ports were added progressively so that round voyages tended to last from four to six months.

Incidentally, the mailbags carried at sea were initially made of hide similarly to those used on mail coaches. But rats had a habit of eating through them, so every Royal Mail ship was required to carry at least one cat to keep down the rats. Later, canvas mailbags were adopted instead.

In its very first full year of trading the company lost two ships through wrecks, one at Turks Island and one near Bermuda. Several more were to suffer similar fates thereafter; in fact five of the original fleet were lost by 1847 through storms and wrecking. One of the original steamships, *Tweed*, was lost with seventy-two lives in February 1847; she had left Havana on the evening of 9th February and struck the Alacranes Reef off Yucutan three nights later, where, rolling in cross seas, she broke up. But, in an epic story of survival and rescue, the survivors built a raft from the wreckage. They were able to take turns in resting on this, while others on the partially submerged reef held the raft off the rocks. A small gig was also salved from the wreckage. Ten souls who set off to seek help in this boat were fortunate to be found by the Spanish brig *Emilio* and taken to the port of Sisal in Yucutan, where canoes were obtained and towed back to the wreck by the *Emilio*. There another sixty-nine were rescued from the raft.

An immediate replacement for *Tweed* was found in none other than Brunel's *Great Western*, which was at that time laid up at Bristol, having, by 1846, completed thirty-seven transatlantic round voyages.

A mail contract for South America was finally signed by RSMP in July 1850 and the first vessel engaged on this route was the *Esk*, a small two-masted schooner with auxiliary propulsion.

In 1851 the largest British paddle-steamer built up to that time, the 2256-gt RMS *Amazon*, 316ft long and 73ft in width over the paddle boxes, was built by R&H Green of Blackwall, at a cost of £100,000. She sailed from Southampton on her maiden voyage on 2nd January 1852 with mails and a valuable cargo of specie and coinage plus mercury for mining in Mexico. She had 109 crew and 50 passengers, in addition to the Captain and two agents. That same night, heading into a strong wind and bad weather, she hove to off Portland Bill but the paddle shafts were overheating. Despite greasing the bearings and hosing down the paddle shafts throughout the next day, flames broke through the boiler casing in the early hours of 4th January. The engineer on duty tried to reach the controls to shut off the engine but was beaten back by the flames. Within minutes the midship section of the hull became a wall of fire even as the ship's engines drove her at full speed into the gale. The Captain turned the ship round to protect the fifty passengers assembled aft but this left most of the crew trapped forward. With the ship still surging forward at something like 9 knots it became almost impossible to get away in the boats, which were capsized by the speed the ship was making through the water; just three boats were, however, successfully launched and by 0400 the burning ship slid beneath the waves. The Captain, who pushed the last boat clear of the ship with his clothes on fire, and 57 others were saved, but 36 passengers and 68 crew, including all the officers, were lost.

The Admiralty thereafter conceded that iron hulls were safer and the first iron ship, *Atrato*, was built for the company in 1853.

On 11th August 1854 the original *Thames* took 400 passengers to Queen Victoria's Naval Review at Spithead. This was the first 'cruise' ever undertaken by Royal Mail. In that same year, *Thames*, along with three other of the original paddle-steamers, the *Great Western*, and three newer Royal Mail ships, were commandeered as Crimean War transports, one, the *Severn* being converted into a hospital ship.

In 1866 Royal Mail started carrying mails onward from St Thomas to Colon, whence they proceeded on a four-hour rail journey to Panama City. From there an onward Pacific service took mails to Australia and New Zealand but this service lost money and was abandoned two years later.

In 1864 the first iron-built screw vessel in the Royal Mail fleet, *Douro*, was built at Greenock. She was placed on West Indies service before being introduced to the Buenos Aires run in 1869 but came to a tragic end when, in collision with a Spanish steamer, she sank off Cape Finisterre in 1882 with the loss of five passengers and twelve crew. These were the last passenger fatalities in the fleet until the First World War. The *Douro* had been a real treasure ship and went down with a cargo of 53,000 gold sovereigns. In a daring salvage operation many of these coins, showing the head of the young Queen Victoria were recovered in the 1990s and later marketed at about £120 each.

Earlier, on 29th October 1867 a great hurricane at St Thomas in the West Indies caused havoc of catastrophic proportions. Of sixty vessels in the harbour only two were afloat the following day and one thousand lives were lost. Royal Mail lost three ships, the *Derwent, Wye* and *Rhone*, the last named with 124 lives, while another three company ships were dismasted in the hurricane.

In 1883 the company's last paddle-steamer was sold out of service. And by 1884 a new route joined Brazilian ports with the West Indies and New York. That year business was booming for Royal Mail and the company earned over £787,000, its highest total so far.

In 1888, with the second *Atrato* and three sisterships, *Magdalena*, *Clyde* and the second *Thames*, the company introduced a milestone ship design with a hull more than 400ft long and passenger accommodation in the superstructure rather than below decks. *Atrato* was a twin-funnel steamer from Robert Napier's yard in Glasgow carrying 221 passengers in three classes. For the first time the ship's masts no longer carried yards and sails. The 421ft long *Atrato* was powered by a 1,000-hp triple expansion engine driving a single screw propeller to give a speed of 15 knots. She spent over twenty years on the West Indies service but was sold to the Viking Cruising Co. in 1912, then taken over by the Admiralty as an armed merchant cruiser at the outbreak of the First World War. Renamed HMS *Viknor*, she was employed on the Northern Patrol but was sunk by a mine off Ulster the following year with the loss of all hands. The *Magdalena*, meanwhile, was taken over by the Admiralty as a troopship stationed in the West Indies and the *Thames* was used as a blockship at Scapa Flow at the beginning of the war.

In 1897 RMS *Danube* and *Orinoco* attended Queen Victoria's Diamond Jubilee Naval Review at Spithead, *Danube* conveying a party from the House of Lords. It was at this review that the Parson's steam turbine was dramatically brought to the public's notice as the *Turbinia* dashed up and down between the anchored ships at 35 knots.

In 1899 five Royal Mail ships were used as troop and supply transports at the outbreak of the Boer War and one of these, *Tagus*, took Boer prisoners to India. She was also used as a hospital ship in the 1914–18 war which she survived.

The year 1900 saw the introduction of the company's yellow funnel, which was to remain with Royal Mail ships throughout the life of the fleet. In 1901 the Government-subsidised Imperial Direct Line started sailings from Bristol to the West Indies, providing unwelcome competition and profits fell again at Royal Mail. Also in that year the *Para* suffered a violent gas explosion in her experimental frozen-fruit hold.

A sister to *Tagus*, the *Trent*, spent four months aground off Cartagena in 1909, then redeemed herself the following year by rescuing the crew of the airship *America* 410 miles south-east of Sandy Hook, thus concluding this first ever attempt to cross the North Atlantic by air.

At the outbreak of the First World War the 3,270-gt cargo ship *Teviot* evacuated refugees from Ostend as the Germans entered that city, and acted as a supply ship throughout the war, reverting to Royal Mail service until broken up in 1928.

In 1915, as a naval depot ship, HMS *Trent* mounted operations against the German cruiser *Königsberg* on the Tanganyikan coast. She also survived the war. In 1917 the *Parana*, which had been built in 1904 for the South American meat trade, fought a German submarine for ninety minutes firing over 70 shells in reply to more than 100 from the U-boat. The arrival of a friendly warship caused the U-boat to break off and dive.

During the ensuing war years Royal Mail ships suffered heavy losses, including *Caroni* torpedoed in 1915, *Ebro* mined in 1917, *Tyne* torpedoed 1917, and the *Tamar* captured and sunk in 1915 by the German raider *Kronprinz Wilhelm*, which had also captured, and later scuttled, the *Potaro*.

The 523ft long *Aragon* was the company's first twin-screw liner. With a capacity for a thousand passengers she made her maiden voyage from Southampton to Brazilian ports and the River Plate in 1905. Later, *Aragon* carried troops to the Dardanelles during the First World War and, according to H.W. Leslie's *Royal Mail War Book*, while *Aragon* was still landing troops of the Worcester Regiment on the port side, wounded were coming in over the starboard side. *Aragon* continued to serve as a military headquarters in the Dardanelles but in 1917, having gone for repairs, was torpedoed and sunk in the roadstead outside Alexandria, after being ordered out of the harbour for lack of a berth. A rescuing destroyer was also sunk with great loss of life.

A sistership, the second *Amazon*, sank a U-boat in January 1917 but was not so lucky the following March when she was torpedoed outward bound from Liverpool. All hands were saved, however, as HMS *Moresby* depth-charged the U-52, forcing the submarine to the surface and destroying her.

Launched in 1906 was the slightly larger 11,537-gt *Araguaya*, which had a lifespan of thirty-six years, being used as a Canadian hospital ship in the First World War, returned to Southampton-Buenos Aires service in 1920, then rebuilt as a cruise ship to carry 365 first-class passengers, eventually being sold to a Yugoslavian company in 1930, then to the French Government in 1940 and finally being sunk on 8th November 1942 in the North Atlantic.

A third A-boat of the Amazon class, RMS *Avon*, made her maiden voyage to Brazil and the River Plate in 1907, took on trooping duties in 1914 and was taken over by the Admiralty for conversion to an armed merchant cruiser fitted with eight 6-inch guns and two anti-aircraft guns in 1915.

Renamed HMS *Avoca*, she was based at Vancouver Island for Pacific service, where she took part in the hunt for the German sail raider *Seeadler*. RMS *Avon* reverted to Royal Mail service in 1919 and was finally broken up in 1930.

The first *Asturias* built in 1907, the fifth of the A-class on South American service, was requisitioned in 1914 as a hospital ship but in 1917 was torpedoed in the Channel with the loss of thirty-five lives, although painted in full hospital colours. With her stern blown off she beached at Bolt Head, and was then towed to Plymouth for use as an Admiralty ammunition hulk. Later repurchased by Royal Mail she emerged from a refit at Harland & Wolff as the cruise liner *Arcadian*.

Three famous passenger ships, *Orduna*, *Atlantis* and *Almanzora*, all built at Harland & Wolff, Belfast, were to achieve the remarkable feat of surviving exemplary service through both world wars.

The 15,500-gt passenger–cargo ship *Orduna*, built in 1914, had a complex propulsion system designed to give 15 knots. Triple screws were powered by twin 4-cylinder triple expansion engines exhausting to a steam turbine on the centre shaft. She had no fewer than thirty-six coal furnaces and six double-ended boilers. Her sistership *Orbita* was not completed until after the war.

Initially voyaging to the West Coast of South America with capacity for more than a thousand passengers, the 570ft *Orduna* was soon chartered to Cunard for the New York service. In 1915 she was attacked by a U-boat with both torpedoes and gunfire 30 miles south of Queenstown but escaped. Three years later, in June 1918 she sank a German U-boat by gunfire, but in December that year unfortunately collided with and sank the Elder Dempster ship *Konakry* off the Irish coast. Between the wars she alternated between the Pacific Steam Navigation Company (PSNC) service to South America and Royal Mail's New York service, carrying more then 800 passengers in three classes, having been converted to oil fuel in 1926. Then in 1941 she was taken over as a troopship, along with a sistership, *Orbita*. One other blemish on her record was a collision with *Almanzora*, although without serious damage, while both were in convoy conveying troops to the Western Desert in May 1941 and taking evasive action against the German battleship *Bismarck*. But this was a normal hazard of wartime navigation since closely packed convoy ships were required to steam without navigation lights and make frequent course alterations. *Orduna* was decommissioned in November 1950, being finally broken up after thirty-seven years of service.

The 16,000-gt *Almanzora*, built at Belfast in 1914, was similar to the *Orduna*, with a distinctive tall single funnel amidships. She was designed to carry a thousand passengers, but served as an armed merchant cruiser in the First World War with the 10th Cruiser Squadron, then gave twenty years service on the Southampton to Buenos Aires run. When in September 1939 she left Buenos Aires for home after a farewell party attended by more than two thousand people, she was due to go to the breakers yard but within a month had sailed again packed with passengers fleeing the European war. Over the next few years she sailed almost 300,000 miles carrying service personnel, refugees, prisoners and repatriates between the various theatres of war over four continents, first as a troopship, then a Government emigration ship. This veteran liner was finally sold for breaking up in 1948 after a long and honourable career of thirty-four years. As a tribute, her forecastle bell was installed in Royal Mail's Head Office in Leadenhall Street, London, as a war memorial.

Almanzora's sisterships, *Andes* (later to be named *Atlantis*) and *Alcantara*, were also built by Harland & Wolff in 1913–14, and similarly converted to armed merchant cruisers each with eight 6-inch guns and two 6-pounders. In 1916, leaving the Skagerrack, the two ships engaged the German raider *Greif* which was disguised as a Norwegian merchant ship *Rena* and was apparently carrying timber on deck. *Alcantara* had closed to within 800 yards and sent a boarding party, before the *Greif* dropped deck screens revealing her guns and opened fire, while also attempting to torpedo both ships. In a fierce battle *Alcantara* was sunk with the loss of seventy-two men, but *Greif* was set on fire and also sunk with the help of two RN warships. *Andes* picked up survivors from both *Alcantara* and *Greif*.

This first *Andes* later engaged in North Atlantic convoy work and in 1917 repatriated British submarine crews trapped at Murmansk by the Soviet revolution. In 1919 she was reconditioned as a passenger ship and resumed the River Plate run. Then in 1929, as a refurbished cruise ship, she was renamed *Atlantis*. In August 1939 after a final cruise to the Baltic, in which she wisely failed to call at Hamburg, *Atlantis* was, in her twenty-sixth year, converted for a totally different role as a hospital ship with 400 sick beds and 130 medical staff. Throughout the ensuing Second World War she sailed unarmed and unescorted. At night her girdle of green lights and illuminated red crosses proclaimed her errands of mercy. She was in the thick of the action in the Norwegian campaign and was attacked from the air near Narvik, though probably because she was mistaken for a warship. Among her many errands was carrying wounded from the Western Desert and El Alamein. In October 1943 she successfully engaged in exchanging British and German prisoners under arrangements made by the International Red Cross. She left Glasgow with

The hospital ship *Atlantis* arriving at Liverpool with repatriated British PoWs in 1943.

788 German sick and wounded and was escorted by German naval vessels from the Norwegian coast into Swedish waters en route for Gothenburg. There *Atlantis* took on 790 British repatriates of which many were stretcher cases. She received a great welcome from planes of the Royal Air Force and from ashore as she arrived back in Liverpool on 26th October 1943.

In 1920 Royal Mail acquired the twin-funnelled passenger ship, *Ohio*; she had been built by AG Weser in Germany and was transferred to the company as reparation for war damage. At 18,400 gt and 591ft long, *Ohio* was the largest ship in the company fleet with capacity for more than 1,400 passengers in three classes. She was, however, laid up only thirteen years later.

It was in 1921 that the company's first motor ship, *Lochkatrine*, built by John Brown & Co., Glasgow, entered a joint service with Holland America Line to the Pacific west coast. Two 16-cylinder 4-stroke single-acting engines each developed 6,400 bhp and drove twin screws to give a speed of 12 knots. On the west coast Vancouver service she carried 11,000 tons of cargo and twelve passengers. *Lochkatrine* was eventually lost, torpedoed by a U-boat in the North Atlantic in 1942 with the loss of nine lives.

In 1925 another twin-funnelled cargo–passenger liner, the second *Asturias*, was built by Harland & Wolff at Belfast. Fitted with refrigeration plants for the carriage of meat from the River Plate, she was at the time the largest motor ship in the world. With twin screws the double-acting Harland & Wolff 8-cylinder engines delivered 15,000 bhp for an intended speed of 17 knots. However, bad vibration and poor speeds resulted in her being re-engined in 1934 with Parson's turbines developing a powerful 20,000 bhp to give speeds of 19 knots. The bow was reshaped and the hull lengthened for speed, while the funnels were heightened. In this new state *Asturias* attended the Silver Jubilee Naval Review at Spithead in 1935. However, at the outbreak of war in 1939, she was converted into an Armed Merchant Cruiser, the foremast and forward funnel being removed to improve the arc of fire of her newly fitted anti-aircraft guns. *Asturias* was on South Atlantic Patrol in 1943 when she was torpedoed, but was able to be towed 500 miles to Freetown. She remained there for two years with her engine room flooded and, abandoned by Royal Mail, was taken over by the Government. Towed to Gibraltar to be patched up early in 1945 under Royal Mail management, and then taken to Belfast for repairs, she became a Government emigrant carrier, and in 1953, reinvented as a regular peacetime troopship, repatriated British troops from Korea. In 1957 she was sold for breaking up but played one last part in history by being used at Faslane to represent night shots of the *Titanic* in the film *A Night to Remember*, most of her white troopship hull bring painted black for this performance and her lifeboats cosmetically painted to give the appearance of the clinker-built boats of earlier years.

Her sistership, the second *Alcantara*, built one year later in 1927, similarly sailed to the River Plate and was refitted and re-engined in 1934, also becoming an Armed Merchant Cruiser in 1939. Initially armed with just a 4-inch gun, she was proceeding to Malta for further arming when she was in collision with Cunard's *Franconia* while zigzagging and went to Alexandria for emergency repairs. New armament comprised eight 6-inch guns, and both the forward funnel and mainmast were removed to give a clear arc of fire for new anti-aircraft guns. Like her sistership, she was on Atlantic Patrol when in July 1940 she sighted a Swedish ship which turned out to be the German raider *Thor*. In the ensuing exchange of fire *Alcantara* was holed on the waterline, which forced her to reduce speed and transfer bunker fuel to the port tanks to raise the shell hole above the starboard waterline. By that time *Thor* had escaped. *Alcantara* was converted to a troopship in 1943, but returned to commercial service for Royal Mail in 1948. After making her final voyage (No.172) in April 1958 she was sold to Japan for scrapping.

In 1927 Royal Mail acquired the shares of White Star Line, a move by the Chairman Lord Kylsant to keep that line as a client of the Belfast ship-builder Harland & Wolff, which Kylsant had also taken over. By the end of 1928, with holdings in several other shipping companies, the Royal Mail Group was the largest shipping and shipbuilding organisation in the world with a fleet totalling more than 2.7 million grt. But the Royal Mail Steam Packet Co. had over-extended itself. There were serious inadequacies in a prospectus to raise more money; financial scandals followed in 1929, Lord Kylsant was disgraced, and the group was then reconstructed. In 1932 Royal Mail Lines Ltd was formed to take over the assets of Royal Mail Steam Packet Co. along with the Nelson and MacIver lines. In this way Nelson Line's five newly built 14,000-ton *Highland* boats joined the Royal Mail fleet.

During the Second World War all the company's vessels were engaged in some official capacity and twenty Royal Mail ships were lost to enemy action. Among the most notable cargo ship casualties was the 5,400-gt *Pampas* built in 1940 but sunk in 1942 during the siege of Malta. She arrived at the island after being viciously attacked and damaged by dive-bombers but her naval gunners had shot down at least one aircraft with her 4-inch and 12-pounder guns; she was then bombed to destruction while unloading in Grand Harbour, having been hit no fewer than eighteen times. A sistership, *Pardo*, was damaged by bombing in Liverpool in 1940 but survived. In 1944 a second *Pampas*, named to commemorate the ship lost in Malta, was converted into a head-quarters infantry landing ship for 650 men. She carried eighteen landing craft on two tiers of davits and took part in the Normandy landings. Renamed HMS *Persimmon*, the same ship took part in the landings on the Irrawady Delta and capture of Rangoon in 1945. She survived and was refitted for commercial service in 1946.

There were many epic stories of bravery and endurance by masters, officers and crews of merchant ships during the Second World War, none more remarkable than on the Arctic convoys. Altogether there were seventy-five convoys to Murmansk and Archangel, in which more than 3,000 British forces and merchant seamen lost their lives as the Allies supplied the Russians with some 7,000 warplanes, 5,000 tanks, tens of thousands of trucks and a vast quantity of soldiers' equipment. Merchant ships from a wide spectrum of shipping companies took part in this 'Hell Run' under escort from the Royal Navy. In addition to the terrible weather, they had to face German surface raiders and U-boats as well as the Luftwaffe based in northern Norway. Many of the cargo ships on these convoys were Government-owned but manned by Merchant Navy personnel. Of particular note is the voyage of the Government cargo vessel *Empire Tide*, managed by Royal Mail, which sailed, under the command of Captain F.W. Harvey, with the famous P.Q.17 North Russian convoy.

On 27th June 1942, P.Q.17, a convoy of thirty-four merchant ships, sailed from Iceland bound for Archangel with guns, tanks and aircraft desperately needed for the eastern front. Of these ships, twenty-two were American, nine British, two Russian and one Dutch. There had already been twenty-five merchant ships lost on the North Russian route during the first half of that year, so P.Q.17 was given strong Royal Navy protection by cruisers, destroyers, corvettes and two converted anti-aircraft ships. In one of these, *Pozarica*, sailed the well-known writer Godfrey Winn who subsequently wrote *P.Q.17*, the definitive and harrowing story of the convoy. If there was one omission in this book it was that there was no specific reference to *Empire Tide* since, following the eventual scattering of the convoy, she was left to make her own way to Archangel. However, in his book *Eight Bells* T.A. Bushell covers *Empire Tide*'s heroic voyage thoroughly, and it is worth summarising here.

The *Empire Tide* was specifically fitted out for her task as an armed but fully loaded merchant ship. She carried one 4-inch low-angle anti-submarine gun, one 12-pounder, four Oerlikon and three twin-Marlin AA guns, with further protection from a balloon, kites and rockets. A Sea Hurricane with catapult launching gear was also shipped on the foredeck, but once launched it would be unable to return to the ship. She carried in her holds a lethal cargo of planes, tanks, guns and ammunition.

From Iceland the convoy set course to pass south of Spitzbergen but an enemy reconnaissance aircraft was soon circling the convoy. The story recounted by Captain Harvey goes that one destroyer officer signalled the aircraft asking it to go round the other way as the seamen were getting dizzy watching him. Without hesitation the pilot duly obliged. Be that as it may, directed by the circling aircraft, large formations of torpedo bombers bore in during the day of 4th July, skimming over the merchant ships at bridge level 'like huge dragonflies'. Several ships were torpedoed but *Empire Tide*'s 12-pounder scored at least two hits as planes fell into the sea. The ship was little damaged, though one gunner was badly wounded. Then a Walrus aircraft delivered a shock message from the Admiralty ordering the convoy to scatter at speed as German battleships were approaching. The main fleet of escorting destroyers drew off to the west, leaving just the converted escorts and armed trawlers to shepherd merchant ships and pick up survivors. Much controversy subsequently raged over this order which resulted in the decimation of the convoy, many of the merchantmen running into packs of waiting German submarines.

Trailing her protective balloon, *Empire Tide* sailed north until in latitude 77° N she reached the ice barrier with its protecting fog banks. Three American ships escorted by an armed trawler are reported to have shown great initiative by sailing through the ice pack undetected while camouflaged overall with white paint, eventually reaching Archangel. Meanwhile *Empire Tide*, under radio orders, steered east towards the Admiralty Peninsula, a northwestern tip of the Russian island of Novaya Zemlya, where, although no observations were possible, a direct landfall was successfully made. Utterly wearied from being on continuous action stations, there being no darkness at that time of year, the Master searched for an anchorage but went aground on this poorly charted inhospitable coast. Floated off by pumping ballast tanks and using her engines the ship then set course for Archangel to the south. But on the morning of 7th July she encountered three enemy submarines, one of which sank a ship ahead, the *Alcoa Ranger*, so *Empire Tide* was forced to reverse course at speed and managed to shelter in a bay on Novaya Zemlya where there was a meteorological station and a small settlement of trappers. There the Captain radioed the Soviet authorities. Meanwhile, the ship's stores now being extremely low, the crew went ashore to collect birds eggs from the cliffs.

Later a Russian Catalina aircraft arrived in the bay bringing medical help, and telling the *Empire Tide* that she had already been reported sunk by the Germans and that a local coaster had been sent to look for survivors of the convoy. On 14th July a coaster did arrive with forty-one survivors from the American ships, *Alcoa Ranger* and *Olopana*. Two days later the coaster brought 107 survivors from four sunken ships, with six of their lifeboats in tow. Many of the rescued men were in a pitiable condition and had to be taken to the settlement, a difficult task over rocky terrain as the ship had but two stretchers. The *Empire Tide* now had a hundred men in excess of her complement. Dwindling food supplies were supplemented by eating birds and fishing; meanwhile to provide water lifeboats from the American ships were used to bring first snow, then fresh water aboard from a local lake.

On the 19th the corvette *La Malouine* entered harbour and instructed Captain Harvey to leave the next day. The corvette brought provisions, gave further medical help and took off eighteen of the castaways. So, after fourteen days in the desolate bay, *Empire Tide* sailed away in the pale light of the midnight sun. She joined a small convoy of five others and reached Archangel in three days without further incident. There, cargo was discharged, but far from being welcomed, the officers and crew were restricted by guards with fixed bayonets. When a naval rating was refused permission to bring some crew mail on board this was too much for the Captain who shut off all power, leaving planes and ammunition hanging from the ship's derricks. He pointed out to the Commissar what hardships the Merchant Navy had gone through to get the cargo to Archangel. Restrictions were then lifted and men allowed ashore while unloading continued.

After discharging her cargo, *Empire Tide* loaded potash and cotton at White Sea ports before sailing for home on 13th September 1942, each ship on the convoy doubling up their complements to bring home survivors. The homeward convoy was again fiercely attacked by aircraft and submarines but did not break formation, although some ships were lost. On 26th September *Empire Tide* arrived home at Loch Ewe, one of only two British merchantmen to return from Convoy P.Q.17. The BBC immediately broadcast the award of decorations by His Majesty: to Captain Harvey the Distinguished Service Order – the first grant of a DSO to the Master of a merchant ship – and to Mr Leech, Chief Officer, the DSC. Several others among the crew were also honoured in the following New Year Honours.

There are also many stories of extraordinary voyages in open lifeboats. One such, concerns the 8260-gt *Nebraska*, one of three sister cargo ships all built at Belfast for Royal Mail in 1919–20 and all three sunk by submarines in the Second World War.

In the spring of 1944 *Nebraska* left Gibraltar with a convoy in ballast to load a full cargo of meat at Buenos Aires. Off Freetown, Sierra Leone, the convoy dispersed and she proceeded independently. Then on 8th April, some 800 miles east of the Brazilian coast, she was torpedoed twice in rapid succession at 0450 and the order was given to abandon ship. Three boats, under the Captain, Chief Officer and Second Officer, got away safely as did two rafts. When the ship had broken in two and sunk, the Second Officer, Mr Allason-Jones (with whom I was later to serve as Third Mate when he was Master of the *Brittany* in July 1957), being in No.3 motor lifeboat, collected the men from the rafts. Two engineers had been killed in the engine room but a roll-call revealed that the full complement of sixty-five were still present; this, it turned out, because the count included two stowaways who had hoped for a quick voyage to South America!

At sunset all three boats set sail for the Brazilian coast but became separated during the night. On the following morning No.3 boat sighted a plane and attracted its attention with smoke floats. Thereafter a Catalina also appeared and at 0610 on 11th April SS *Kindat* came alongside and took the rescued men to Freetown. But Captain Dodds' boat was not so lucky. Although sighted by an American plane which dropped a message giving a course to reach Pernambuco, he had expected a rescue ship to be sent out but had to sail on, after making repairs to the rudder. During the next few days, with a fair wind but rather rough sea, they made about 3 knots, before the gaff on the mainsail split in two, reducing the sail area considerably. Nonetheless, on the fourteenth day the Captain with unerring navigation steered his boat straight into the harbour of Recife, Pernambuco. According to Captain Dodds, 'Apart from a certain weakness in the legs all the boat's crew were in good health on landing.'

The Chief Officer, Mr Buckney, also brought his No.2 boat safely to the Brazilian coast on the very same day, 22nd April. He was a veteran, having previously been torpedoed and spent ten days in an open boat. According to the *Nebraska's* Assistant Purser, Mr K.D. Lamb, on their second day they spotted planes on three occasions. However, releasing smoke floats and using a flashing mirror, which formed part of every boat's equipment, failed to attract attention. Food stored in the boat included biscuits, pemmican, Horlicks tablets, and chocolate, some lime juice and rationed water. The boat made good progress, however, blown by the south-east trade wind. If the ship had been torpedoed a little further north, in the doldrums, it would have been a different story. For the first eight days the boat kept up a good average of about 100 miles a day. Then the wind became variable and died, so that on the eleventh day the sail was lowered and the men allowed to bathe, one at a time. At sunset of the twelfth day a piece of floating wood marked 'Swift', brand name of the South American meat company, gave them hope that they were in the shipping lane off the Brazilian coast, and the sight of a butterfly at dusk was cause for further optimism. The next day came seaweed and a change in the colour of the sea. The Chief Officer estimated that they had now run 1,130 miles; double rations of water were allowed. At 0730 on the fourteenth day land was sighted, but the roar of breaking surf was also heard. Later a seaplane came and dropped provisions with a message that the nearest town was 10 miles south. But they were being drawn into the shore and stood off for an uncomfortable night during which they rowed hard to keep head to sea. The following morning they pulled hard through tumbling waters to beach the boat, coming safely ashore at 0745 on the coastline midway between Recife and Bahia, there to be welcomed by native Indians.

The *Highland* ships, built in Belfast between 1928 and 1930, became well known around the world for their unique appearance characterised by a split accommodation block and squat twin funnels. One, the *Highland Patriot*, was a war casualty lost in 1940, torpedoed by a U-boat while homeward bound from the Plate with meat and general cargo. Initially the four remaining *Highland*s continued to bring refrigerated meat to the UK but were taken over in 1941 by the Admiralty as troopships, each with cargo decks converted to give capacity for some 1,250 men. They set out on a series of voyages to South Africa and Suez, sometimes being rerouted home via the River Plate for cargo. Later their capacity was greatly increased to move US troops to North Africa and Great Britain. As the war in Europe ended, the *Brigade*, *Chieftain* and *Monarch* were ordered east to the Japanese war, taking part in the reconquest of Burma and Malaya, later repatriating prisoners of war from the Far East.

The passenger ships which survived the Second World War, and whose distinguished histories are separately described in this chapter, included *Atlantis*, *Almanzora*, *Asturias*, *Alcantara* and the second *Andes*, as well as the four *Highland* ships. All were engaged at the end of the war in trooping, repatriation or hospital ship duties.

In 1946, among her other duties, *Atlantis* carried, from Southampton to their husbands in Australia, 450 war brides with 135 children, most of them less than a year old. Another of her 'cargoes' comprised a large number of Italian brides joining their Polish husbands in the UK. It was as well that the ship was still fitted out for hospital work as one or two babies were born every day of the voyage from Naples! Thereafter chartered for four years by the Government to carry emigrants from Southampton to Australia and New Zealand, this fine old lady was finally laid up for scrap in the Clyde in 1952. Meanwhile the *Highland* boats had re-entered the South American service in 1947–48 after repatriating troops and prisoners between the continents.

A German passenger ship, *Ubena*, built by Blohm & Voss, Hamburg, in 1928 and taken over in 1939 by the German Navy, became the mothership to U-boat flotillas. Having surrendered to Great Britain in July 1945, she was renamed *Empire Ken* and operated by Royal Mail as a prominent troopship until 1957.

Built by Harland & Wolff in 1939 and to become Royal Mail's flagship and later a well-known cruise ship, the 26,000-ton passenger liner *Andes* had been launched just before the outbreak of the Second World War and was due to make her maiden voyage to South America on 26th September 1939, the one-hundredth anniversary of the founding of Royal Mail. Instead she was ordered to Liverpool where she was converted to a troopship with a capacity for more than 4,000 men. Her wartime career was remarkable: she twice circumnavigated the globe, carrying troops worldwide, and played her part in the North African landings, all without untoward incidents of any kind. At the conclusion of hostilities she had the distinction of returning the Norwegian Government to Oslo.

The *Andes*, as flagship of the RML fleet, finally made her first commercial voyage to South America in 1948. But she was again converted, this time for cruising in 1959, to carry 480 passengers in one class. She became a very popular cruise ship with a reputation for good service during the early 1960s but was finally broken up in 1971 after thirty-one years of service.

In 1949 a new 17,500-ton passenger liner, *Magdalena*, built as replacement for the *Highland Patriot*, sailed on her maiden voyage to South America, but in one of Royal Mail's most embarrassing episodes, went aground due to a navigational error when approaching Rio de Janeiro on the homeward leg of that maiden voyage. She broke in two and had to be scrapped.

Meanwhile RML's long-time steady sugar trade from Cuba, one of the mainstays of the West Indies run, had been cut off by Fidel Castro following the revolution.

In 1959–60 the three new white-hulled A-boats, *Amazon*, *Aragon* and *Arlanza*, came into service as replacements for the *Highland* class. These were the last ships to be built for Royal Mail. They were of another unique design and remarkable for their diverse roles; they could carry 107 first-class, 82 cabin-class and 275 third-class passengers, each class with its own public rooms, catering facilities, open deck areas and tiled swimming pool. With five cargo hatches and four cargo decks, a large proportion of hold space was given over to chambers for carrying chilled and frozen meat homeward from the River Plate. There were also strong rooms for carrying bullion, and lockers for mailbags and baggage. Deck cargo was frequently loaded by the ships own cranes and this would include passenger cars being taken on the three to four-day trip to and from the UK to Vigo and Lisbon. Emigrants for Brazil and Argentina were carried outward in third class and for this purpose additional Spanish and Portuguese catering crew were taken on in these ports.

Launched by HRH Princess Margaret in July 1959 RMS *Amazon* made her maiden voyage in January 1960, shortly to be followed by *Aragon* and *Arlanza*. This proud trio made regular sailings to South America for the best part of a decade. However Royal Mail's meat trade was dealt a devastating blow by an outbreak of foot-and-mouth in Argentina. Also passenger air travel and air mail gradually encroached on the A-ships' custom during the 1960s; people no longer found time for three-week voyages to or from South America, emigration to Brazil and Argentina had peaked, while mail was increasingly sent by air, so inevitably these labour-intensive ships gradually became uneconomic as all their principal functions had failed within a decade.

In 1965 Furness Withy acquired the share capital of Royal Mail, having already absorbed Shaw Savill & Albion, thus bringing together one of the largest British shipping groups, and from then on many ships were interchanged between the services of these companies. The three A-ships, being unable to pay their way, were, in 1968, transferred to Shaw Savill's Australian service, but this was commercially unsuccessful, and Furness Withy sold them off among twenty-three ships including the flagship *Andes* in 1970, thus marking the end of Royal Mail's passenger services, as the ships were finally taken over by the Hong Kong shipowner C.Y. Tung. The A-ships were ignominiously sold for conversion to car carriers, and by 1972 Royal Mail Line had effectively ceased to exist as a separate entity.

Reader's Guide to Selected Nautical Terms

Cargoes:

LNG: Liquid natural gas.

LPG: Liquid petroleum gas.

TEU: Twenty-foot equivalent units, used to measure container capacity in ships.

Tramp ship: Available for charter to shippers for individual cargoes or on 'Time Charter'.

Ship's engines:

Bunkering: Taking on fuel.

Horse-power (hp): Engine's rate of doing work. In metric units 1hp = 745.7W.

Brake horse-power (bhp): Engine power measured at the crankshaft after allowing for frictional losses. *Shaft horse-power (shp)* is measured close to the propellers.

Screw propellers: Introduced from the 1860s to supersede paddles.

Turbo-electric drive: The ship's turbine drives an electric generator which in turn drives a motor to turn the propeller shaft.

Floating conditions:

Draft/draught: Depth of water under the keel.

Freeboard: Height amidships between deck and waterline.

Trim: Difference between drafts forward and aft.

Ship structure:

Amidships: The mid-point of the length of a ship's hull.

Bilge: Rounded corner between vertical and bottom shell plating.

Bulkhead: Vertical partition in a ship.

Bulwark: Steel plating to rail height along the ship's sides. Water is drained from decks through scuppers in the bulwarks.

Catwalk/Flying Bridge: Raised walkway on a tanker between forecastle, midship and aft accommodation.

Cowls: Vent openings to assist circulation of air below deck.

Deckhead: Horizontal ceiling to a space.

Forecastle: Raised deck at the bow.

GRP: Glass reinforced plastic used in boat construction.

Hatch Coamings: Vertical plates 2-3 feet high surrounding the cargo hatchways.

Midship section: Transverse section of the ship's hull amidships.

Hawse pipe: Tunnel (on either side of bow) through which the anchor chains run.

Poop: Deck space at the stern.

Stabilisers: Fins extended on either side of the hull, usually one pair amidships, to reduce ship's rolling. These are gyro-controlled to anticipate the rolling motion of the hull.

Tweendeck: Cargo deck below the weather deck running the length of the cargo holds.

Ship's equipment:

Accommodation ladder: A ladder which can be raised or lowered along the ship's side for access to boat or quayside.

Azimuth mirror: Prism set over a compass to measure horizontal bearings of terrestial or celestial objects.

Binnacle: Brass cover over the magnetic compass which is standard requirement in any ship.

Falls: Ropes rove through blocks used to lower or raise lifeboats.

Ship's bell: On the forecastle, heavy brass with ship's name engraved in it. At night in open seas the look-out would ring the bell once for a light seen to starboard, twice when seen to port and three times for dead ahead. Traditionally, in the past, the bell had been rung every half-hour to mark the four-hour watch from 'one-bell' to 'eight bells'.

Telegraph: Handle operated brass stand with dials to transmit orders from bridge to engine room in steps from 'full ahead' to 'full astern'.

Voice-pipes: Simple air pipes (capped with whistles) for speaking directly between navigating bridge, Captain's cabin and engine room.